INTANGIBLE ORGANIZATIONAL RESOURCE STRATEGY

JOHN LOK

Contents

Contents

Preface

Introduction

Any organizations must need resources to be provided in order to suppky for their organizational development. However, resouces may include human resources, equipment facilities resources , earth natural resource e.g. land, water wood, gas et. building material resources, even working time resources , technological etc. different kinds of resources. Thus, it scems that any organizations must need some resources to help their organizational daily operation in success.

The question concerns what the best resources used strategies to be achieve the most efficiency or the best performance to be organizational development.

In my these series, I shall explain what factors may influence an organizations to use that resources in the most efficient effectiveness in order to avoid to waste nature or human or material resources . Readers can learn what the strategies may be applied to avoid organizational wasting resource behaviors. In my this book four series, I shall apply how and why organization resource shortage can bring what influence to organizational and social change.

How can business apply right or reasonable science management principle to manage that businesses effectively and efficiently in order to achieve sale and profit raising aim in the least resource suitation? Otherwise, applying wrong or unreasonable science management principle , it can bring what disadvantages or negative impacts to the businesses. IN my this chapter, I shall attempt to indicate above questions . Readers can have more clear view whether why the kinds of science resource management methods are not suitable to be applied to the kind of organizations to bring negative impact consequences.

Prologue

profit or e-books or paper books sale ability. p.61-75

● How mental (managerial) accounting concept helps Amazon publish to make investment decision?

● Can robots perform management accounting analysis tasks

● Why does organizational resource budget need?

● How can the laptop computer seller applies management accounting data to analyze whether which is the main factor to influence laptop buyer behavior changes?

Chapter 5

The relationship between resource shortage and consumer behavior

Can resource shortage influence consumer behavior changes? p.76-85

Can bring either positive or negative or both impact to change consumer behavior when the consumer begins to feel resource shrtage occurrence to choose to buy the kind of product or consume the kind of service?

How does a consumer make choice with scarce resources?

Do they have relationship between organizational technology resource economic behavior and social needs?

Why have they interaction to influence resource supply between orgaizations and societies?

Chapter 6

Ecommerce organization resource management strategy

Why does in this e-commerce organization situation, online webstore speed must be the most important factor to influence its sale success. Information technology internet speed, online webstore design, online transation convenience transaction feeling (tangibale and intangible both resource factors) may influence its future clients number ? p.86-105

How an ecommerce organization resource affects ssociety?
Why has online webstore's information technology resource close relationship to influence online buyers number and social job chance?
How do organizational resources affect organizational change?
How to build organizatonal resource using right psychology
How psychological method help employees to avoid resource waste

Chapter 7
OUTSOURCING SERVICE RESOURCE AVOID WASTE STRATEGY

●

●

Outsourcing or insourcing in human resource
supply chain factor
●

Global outsourcing source strategy
in a value supply chain
●

Outsourcing benefits in economic view
●

What motivate outsourcing and what is being
outsourced risk and concerns?
●

How can choose smarter outsourcing?
●

What is environmental uncertainty factor?

●

Whether outsourcing will bring
what kind of work skills.

● Bibliography

- What are entertanment theme park intangible resource
- How intangible resource excites visitors entertainment need

  Entertainment theme park resources supply and leisure player psychology relationship
- What are entertanment theme park intangible resource
- How intangible resource excites visitors entertainment need p.204-218

Explaining the relationship between increasing proficient workers number and avoiding excess resource waste
- In organizational behavioral economic view, whether they have cause and effect relationship between employees how to use resources behaviors and organizational resource excess use within organizations ? p.219-225

- green building avoids resource waste p.220-226
- facility management helps organizations to avoid resource waste

ONE

INTERNET INTANGIBLE TECHNOLOGY KNOWLEDGE RESOURCE

New economy brings new way of resource management. The old loyalty and job security -based organization changes, organizations know that the assets are largely made up employees (HRM), but many new organizations begin to believe technology is important assets, such as Amazon is global ecommerce delivery service organization. It seems internet high technology is its important intangible resource to help it earn global e-buyers number increases . So , many organizations began to believe that technology will be important resource, such as internet can provide online business chance. With all the businesses are taking full advantage of internet, for example, the US department estimates that the value of retail e-commerce in 2000 year was about $25 billion, which represents less than 1% of US retail sales. Despite this, interest in e-business remains high.

● Why internet may be main technology resource to organizations?

E-commere needs strategy in order to win competitors, questions include: What criteria do customers use to choose between our firms and competitors? How do the best employees decision whether to join? What business environment attracts and keeps the best suppliers making with our firms? What characteristics draw the most royal invesdtors to our firms? e.g. Amazon . com's web site and Wal-mart's can apply internet technology resource to create each e-store to let e-buyers to choose any kinds of products to buy athome conveniently. Hence, internet technology, even future other kinds of new technology may be main technology resources to organizations, when they can help organizations to raise sale competitive effort.

I mean that digital economy will be one kind new digital resource to future any organizations. The essential piece is the knowledge, it is what give it life and what makes it an interesting and fulifulling purchase and sale channel for people to spend their time , such as e-commerce virtual organization may be leaded to let purchase and ale transactions carry on easily from online websites. Hence, internet may be main knowledge management (intellectual capital) resource to any e-commerce organizations. It is about the storage, transfer knowledge.

For Amazon publish example, e-books will be knowledge as an object, like a book in library. Amazon can apply internet technology to help it to sell any author's ebooks from its book estores. So, ebooks are Amazon's knowledge resources to help it to create readers incomes. E-books is intangible knowledge resource to Amazon . Any authors' paper and ebooks will be sold cheap price to help Amazon to attract global readers to choose to buy its ebooks from its different countries e-webstores at home conveniently.

Hence, any e-commerce organizations also need HRM (emanagers) to help them to deliver a superior value (world class capabilities) in both te virtual and physical world. E-management will be another main human resources to e-commerce organizations. Why does e-management will be future main HRM resource to e-commerce organization? The reasons may include:

E-management demands in sort of managerial/e-commerce sale strategy effort, skills at positioning the firm within a networm of industries, e-management also demands the ability to see how the firm fits into a value creation-e-management is different because doing it work requires the e-engineering of business eco-systems, e-management demands the ability to be connected to thousands of inputs about specific changes among many industry participants , such as suppliers , customers, employees, competitors, media and shareholders.

Effective e-management requires the ability to monitor developments that can change with unusually high frequency. However, it is also essential that e-managers distinguish between the few meaningful inputs and the many inputs that have limited significance, ability to sustain organizational change, effectie e-managers monitor changes in their markets. So, instead of e-commerce organizations need to employ talent e-managment staffs to help them to manage overall e-commerce organizations. E-leading staffs (HRM) is another main HRM need. E-leaders need to know how to design online brochures, e.g. online brochures simply involved putting a company's market materials on the web. in order to attract or persuade online buyers visit its websites and choose the most right price of product to buy easily. E-leaders need to lead front-office transactions which involved putting customer facing customers , such as placing on order on the web when leaving back-office activities, such as order fulfillment unchanged.

E-leaders also need to integrate online online purchase transactions in which a firm actually linked its front -office and back -office systems and processes in a fashion, e.g. most companies have developed online brochures , in order to let online advertisement tool to attract e-buyer individual purchase choice from its webstores. Hence, future any e-commerce organizations must need (HRM (e-leaders and e-managers) to help them to bring innovation in order to achieve maximize profit aim. So, internet webstores, e-leaders , e-managers may be future e-commerce organization main resources. So, e-commerce organizations, manages are actors at three levels: In the front line , as entrepreneurs, in the middle , as facilitators, and integrators, at the top as institution builders.

Hence, future new economical society, it creates e-commerce organizations number increases, when consumers began to accept online purchase transaction activities. Hence, it causes e-commerce began to feel internet (e-webstores, e-leaders, e-managers), they will be the most influential resources (intangible knowledge managment and tangible URM both resourcees to influence their success or failure.

● Why doe e-commerce organization believe (e-webstore

design, e-leaders and e-managers) will be main organizational resources?

The most important question: It asks when e-buyers visit their webstores, wo are their target customers and shich needs of theirs are their trying to satisfy? For exap,e many airlines , e.g. American airlines, China airlines began to feel online e-tickets sale channel is more easily than paper ticket shop sale channel, because many air passengers began to accept e-ticket/online ticket purchase choice more than visiting airline shops . They feel that they do not want to waste time to visit airline shops. They like to pre-book to buy e-ticket to pay from the airline e-websote conveniently. Hence, e-webstore design knowledge management , e-leaders and e-management webstore management skill will be future any one e-commerce organizations their main tangible and intangible resources (assets) to help their e-commerce businesses development.

On conclusion, I believe that the current economy is not a high-tech economy or an internet economy, not an m-commerce economy , but instead customer econoomy. Customers need to gather with information and access, they are demanding, fair, global price, they are demanding that compares deal with them using the distribution channel , they choose manufacturing direct and through dealers and retailers. Base on those factors, they encourage future many e-commerce organizations cause organization change traditional resouce concept, such as land, capital equipment, tangible resource began to change to e-commerce organization's intangibel and tangible resource, such as knowledge management to e-online web store design skills, e-leaders and e-managers e-stores sale management strategy and e-buyer product research and brochure online advertisement design skill. All of these knowledge management skill will be future organizations' main resources to help them to create new economic competition effort.

TWO

ORGANIZATION RESOURCES

What are organizational resources ? What do organizational resources mean? What kinds of organizational resources are needed? What negative impact may be influenced if organizations lack enough resources to influence organizational development? Does working time belong to organizational time resources to influence employee individual efficiency e.g. how arranging enough employee to do the identified task in the most short time in order to achieve the most efficient performane? I shall attempt to identify examples to explain above questions as below:

In general, organizational resources are all assets, that are available to a firm for use during the production process. The four basic types of organizational resources are human, monetary , raw materials and capital. Organizational resources are combined, used and transofrmed to finished products during the production process. For organizational human resource example, human resource activities full under the following five core functions: staffing, development, compensation, safety and health core functions.

● HR resource

HR conducts a wide variety of activities. However, in any organizations, the major resources used by organizations are often described as follow (1) human resources (2) financial respirces (3) physical resources and (4) information resources. Managers are responsible for acquring and managing the resources to accomplosh goals. Hence, in organizational HR aspect, it may include these function, such as retirement and selection, performance management , learning and development, succession planning, compensation and benefits, human resource information systems. Because considering that for many organizations employees themselves represent a significant cost to the business, if the organization can use its employees in efficiency.

Then, it can avoid human resource in excess or in surplus on wasting challenge. Then , its employee cost or salary can be reduced. I t means that it does not need to employ in excess employees number, but the organization can still achieve itself the most efficient performance. Hence, any organizations must need to learn how to avoid " in excess employees number supply or wasting employee working behaviors" challenge . Because if some tasks do not need many employees to work together, it can still be achieved efficiency . Then , the organization ought not employee too many or excess employees to finish the kind of task. Thus, learning how to use efficient human resources, it can help organizations to avoid wasting working time to any departments employees. For example, when one factory has limited land to be supplied to become warehouse in order to help it to keep sticks. If it has excess logistic or factory workers number. Then, they are wasting working time to do not important tasks in warehouse, it means that if the factory has only one warehouse, but its area is small, it can allow maximum 50 workers to stay in the warehouse , but the warehouse has above 100 workers are staying to deliver goods in the small warehouse . Then, they must not actieve the most efficiency , even their delivery or transport goods performance will be influenced to worse by noise and crowd warehouse working environment. Hence, excess employees number in any working environment, which can not improve organizational performance or riase efficiency any organizations can not neglect " excess employees number" organizatinal HR resource arranging issue.

The solution concerns arranging the most right or the most exact empllyees number in order to supply to any organizational departments. Then, the organization can avoid wasting employee individual talent, reducing employing cost, improvig performance, achieving the most efficiency. Resource capacity means resource pool who are available in the organization to take up to appropriate human resource arrangement to assist any departmental development in long term efficiency. Hence, organizational human rsources may become talent tangible assets or foolish tangible assets. It depends on how the organization's resource capacity tasks arrangement to every employee in different departments. If the organization neglects how to arrange every employee task in the most exact or the most appropriate employees number in the department.

The department's efficiency must be caused worse, because excess employees number, it can not help it to achieve the most efficiency aim, even it may influence the excess employees , themselves feel waste working hours to do the not essential or not important tasks. Then, the organization may cause talent employee to become foolish employee. Otherwise, the organization's efficiency to be worse, because when the department has not enough employees to work. Then , any one employee may feel hard to work, his/her emotion may be influenced to negative, then his/her workig behavior may b inefficiency or lazy working. On consequence, the organization may bring economic loss, due to employee individual lasy working behavior, negative working emotion, even high working pressure may be caused, when one employee needs to do more , then the employee's task, but his/her salary can not increase. He/she will feel unfair to compare the another department employee, he /she does not need to spend long working hours or overtime to work per day. SO, any organization needs to avoid shortage employee supply or excess employee supply issue to any departments. Appropriare employees number is the best strategy in order to raise overall organizational efficiency.

● Time resource

Instead of human resource, land, raw material, earth natural resource, electricity, gas may be organization resources . Whether time may be organizational resources, organizational time management vires time as a scarce resource that must be invested as effectivity. Time is an infinite resource . If not properly managed on in an organization. It can have a negative impact on both employer's and employee's productivity. So, organizations should ensure that workers are well equipped to manage time in their duties.So, in management view, any organization managers must need to consider how to manage time, eg . how to arrange employees to work in different departments in order to achieve the most efficiency. They need to understand which resources are in short supply and focus on the prioritizing work across shared resources, they need agree on a common approach, they also need to realize resource management is an ongoing process. Thus, time is an often ignored but invaluable resource in any organization. All activities be it procurement.

An organization's time, in contrast, goes largely unmanaged. Although, phone calls, email, instant messages , meetings, they are general daily tasks to any organizations managers, but mangers need to know how to arrange the most urgent tasks in prior. For example, if the manager can not arrange a meeting to the discuss client tomorroe, as well as the manager needs to spend two hours to meeting with overall 200 employees to discuss how to solve improving efficiency challenge tomorroe. So, this manager needs to make choice whether he ought spend two hours meeting to the business client, or two hours meeting to 200 employees. If he chooses to meet the business client tomorrow, he will help his firm to win the important business chance, but he can not discuss how to improve efficiency in order to find the best method to let 200 employees to know tomorrow. Thus, tomorrow time management will be one importat time resource to the manager. The manager needs to arrange tomorrow two hours time how to plan business meting or efficiency imporvement meerting either to his 200 employees or the one business client. Because if the manager decided to meet the client, he must need to spend today time to aplan or organize how to arrange either business proposal content for the business client or organizational operational challenge questions and solutions for his 200 employees .

So, today time management is also important time resource to influence tomorrow either the success business meeting or the organizational 200 employees meeting. So, it seems that time management may be one important resource to any managers more than general employees in any organizations.

If the manager can know how to manager his/her time to do any prior tasks, then he/she may help the organization to raise efficiency or improve performance. Otherwise, if the manager can not know how arrange what prior urgent task needs to be finished. Then, worse performance or inefficiency may be influenced to cause. So, if the organization manager can know how to make time arrangement, I believe that he can help the organization employees to raise efficiency more easily.

THREE

ORGANIZATION EFFICIENT USING RESOURCES ECONOMIC METHOD

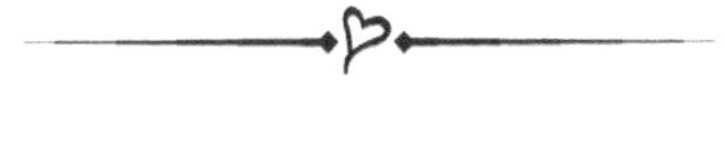

In behavioral economic view , any organizations can attempt to apply behavioral economy method to use resources efficiently. Organizational excellence framework performance measurement takes a systematic approach . One of the most effective ways of using resources and minimizing that use of work. Calculating task cost in the most efficient economic method to help organizations to reduce cost and avoid resources waste, e.g. using resource management software, technology, planning and taking a systematic approach , which aims to manage the most efficient steps to follow to finish or implement each task in the most shor time as well as avoiding excess employees number.

Organizational resource efficiency means using the organization's limited resources in a sustainable manner when minimising impacts on the organization performance. It allows the organization to create more with less and to deliver greater value with less money. HR, raw material, technology input to carry on any organizational resources efficiently ? Management is the process of using organizational resources to achieve organizational goals of using organizational resources to achieve organizational goals effectively and efficiently through planning , organizing , leading and controlling. An efficient organization makes the most productive use of its resource in the most short time and the most eficiency and the least cost aspects.

● What is efficient use of resources to any organizations in economics?

Economic efficiency implies an economic state in which every resource is optimially allocated to serve each individual or entity in the best way when minimizing waste and inefficiency. whan an economy is economically efficient, any changes made to assist one entity would harm another . Hence, budget how much spending on resources, e.g. employee saley, office and/or plant technological equipment facilities , before making resource expenditure spending decision. Budget is essnetial to help the organization to deduce resource using and excess purchase waste since budget and resource of organizations have interlock or interconnet relationship. If the organization can make exact udget, then it can avoid excess expenditure or waste resource to use. So, organizations need to acquire a talented resource pool , that can lead projects to success, when any kinds of resources are achieved to be supplied to use inn enough . For example, using an effective enterprise resource management system that delivers capabilities. Regardless of the approach and tools used, organizations must determine how to balance to use any kinds of resources efficiently. Thus, in organizational efficient resource using behavioral economy view, the organizational efficiency factor means that influences the efficiency of the organization's use if its resources can be both internal and external, e.g. how implementing strategic plans, they may include selecting what methods and resources to use, and leadning employees on guideline, working in coalitions with organizations around to deliver those needs in the most resource efficient way.

In organizational studies, resource managemetn is the efficient and one resource management technique of resource leveling, of finding the answers to the question, how to use available resource efficiently, effectively and economically ot organization resource expense. SO , resource management is the process of allocating resources and allocating.

● What is meant by economic using of resource to organizations?

Economic resources are the factors used in producing goods or providing services. Economic resources can be divied into human resources, such as labors and management, and non humann resource, such as land, capital , goods, finished resources and technology , for example, natural resource is a key input in the production process that stimulates economic growth. Natural resources have limited direct economic use in satisfying human need, but transforming them into goods and services enhances their economic value to the socirty. So, if the country has many organizations know how to use their natural resources input in that production processes. Then, they can create themselves economic benefits directly and attribute economic benefit to society indirectly.

Thus, the types of economic organizations can be identified, there are subsistence recipreocal exchange with subsistence, peasant with primary reliance on self-produced food, but containing some exhange elements, market-commercial , redistribution or state socialist. Thus organizations need to learn hoe to use themselves organizational resources efficiently. Organizational resources are all assets that are to a firm for use during the production process. The four basic types of organizational resources are human, monetary, raw material and capital. Organizational resources are combined , used and transformed into finished products during the production process. So, a business that understands how to use resources efficiently. resource management is the process of allocating resources in order for a company to grow easily.

Organizational economic is used to study transactions within individual firms and determine management approach to managing resources. It is broken down into thee major subjects: agency theory, transaction cost economic and property rights theory. Agency theory is a priinciple that is used to explain and resolve issues in the relationship between business principles and their agents. Most commonly, that relationship is the one between shareholders as principles, and company executives as agents. Agency theory is used to understand the relationship between agents and principals. The agent represents the principal in a particular business transaction and is expected to represent the best interests of the principal without regard for seld interest. So, when the relationship between shreholders and company executives is kept the best.

Transaction cost economic is understood as alternative modes of organizing transactions (governance structure, such as markets, firms and bureaus) that mininize transactions costs. This, cost is the primary determinant of such as firm's decision whether it is the most right (the best) or the worst decision. It will influence the firm ho to spend resource behavior. The cost other than the money price that are incurred in trading good and service. SO, if the organization can often make the best decision to carry on any activites. It will avoid to waste resources efficiently. For example, if transaction cost influces the commission, paid to a stockbroker for completing a share deal and booking fee charges when purchase concert tickets. The cost of travel and time to complete an exhange , it means that transaction cost. So if the organization can make the best or the most reasonable decision to carry on any business activities. Then, its transaction cost can be influenced to reduce the most level in order to bring resources economic benefit. e.g. sunk costs are indpeendent of any event and should not resulting from economic trade in a market.

Property right theory means contracted choice, through ownership, property rights theour clarifies the firm's boundary choice. The maon egal property rights are the right of possession, the righ tof excession. So, for the efficiency of property rights al scarce resources are owned by someone. IN the right property rights approsed to the theory of the firm, I assume that in the case of sale ownership by party-property rights define the theoretical and legal ownership of resources and how resources can be used by organizatin. So, above three major organizational theories can assist organizations to know how to spend resources efficiently.

FOUR

THE RELATIONSHIP BETWEEN ORGANIZATION RESOURCES USING AND SOCIAL RESOURCES

Resources needers may include societies needers ,e.g. government house material householders , electricity , water , natural resources needers, schools, public houses , land number and area needs etc. as well as business organiztions , office building material, office, plant, land area, number need, equipment facilities limited number . So, when global office and plant business users need to buy more land, equipment materials etc. and electricity , water. Social resources number reduces to bring resourcee shortage challenge causes. Have they have shortage relationship (resource demand number is more than supply number) between social resources need and business resource need? I shall attempt to explain this question as below:

I assume global business organization number increases, they will need many natural resources, e.g. water, electricity, gas, land to supply for office, plant building , material and staff office electricity, gas, plant , office daily essential power need. So, when global business organizations number increases, they may need to use much raw material and natural resources for equipment facility, office plant building material, even day office, plant electricity , gas power, staff drinking water etc. basic office operational needs, when global business organizations number increase.

The question concerns whether they will cause natural resources shortage to supply to social need , when global business organizatins number increases. First, I shall explains what social resources needers mean as below:

● Social resource are defined as any concrete or symbolic term that

can be used as an object of exchange among people (Foa & Foa, 1980), money, information, goods and services both tangible items , such as are ususally defined the assessment of social need is of central allocation between organization needers and social citizen needers both stakeholders. So, when global human birth rate and life time increases, population number will increase, then their social resources need are also increasing, if global organizaions and population number are increasing in the same time, due to earth natural resources has limit number to supply in order to satisfy organizations and families daily resources need, e.g. building material resources are used to build either to build offices, plants or private houses , public house, lands resources are used either to build private or public houses or offices , plants , water is supplied to either office staffs drinking or families drinking, electricity , gas resources are limited to supply either offices plants use or families private or public houses use. Hence, due to all of earth, but in the same time, global offices , plants, government organizations and families numbers both stakeholders number is continue increasing. They have possible to encounter natural resources shortage issue when natural resources are using much, but they can nt manufacturers to increase by human easily.

● Can responding to resource scarcity help some kinds business grow?

Foe example, the food and agricultural business organizations, e.g. supermarkets, restaurants, they must send plactic material to manufacture plactic bags to supply to supermarket buyers to carry fruits, breads, mil, etc. foods when consumers need to buy the kinds of foods in any supermarkets, if plactic material supply number is decreasing, then a lot plactic bags can not supply to let buyers to carry their foods, due to plactic bags number is shortage , it will cause any supermarket buyers feel inconvenient when they need plactic bags to carry their foods, they choose to buy the kind of foods from supermarket to themselves homes.

So, if plactic bags manufacture material i shortage, it can not be manufactured to plactic bags to supply to global supermarket organizations. Then, the one supermarket can provide enough plactic bags to let them to carry their foods from supermarkets to themselves homes conveniently. The focus on plactic bag resource scareity is not impossible to occur to supermarket organization case. If families are often using plactic bag to carry rubbish daily at home. Then, plactic bags number can not increase to satisfy global supermarkets food plactic bags and families themselves homes rubbish plactic bags both stakeholders need. Plastic bags can not be manufactured to supply to manufacture lot plactic bags supply to satisfy global families rubbish plactic bags home users and supermarkets food plactic bas users needs. Consequently, plactic bags prices may be influenced to increases, when plactic bags demand increases, but supply decreases. It is one good exaple to explain why plactic bag manufacturered material supply decreases, it may influence plactic bags number decreases and price increases, because families home rubbish plactic bags and supermarket food plastic bags need both increase.

Consequence, supermarket cost may be influenced , due to plastic bags number also increase much, if one day shortage of plactic manufacturing material supply number is shortage. So, it seems that food plastis bags using number, they have close relationship to impact supermarket food plastic bags price, if supermarkets lack enough plastic bag number supplies, then they need to increase food price, even the supermarket may lose customers , if it can not supply plastic bags to let them to use the supermarket itself plastic bags to carry fruits, ,ilk, soft drinks conveniently. Hence, plastic bag material may be one kind of important natureal resource for supermarkets, because any one consumer may be influenced to choose another supermarket when he/she feels the another supermarket can supply plastic bags to let him/her to carry on fruits, milks, soft drinks conveniently.

Another kind of natureal resource , such as steel material for restaurants , steel material can help global restaurants to manufacture kniefs, glass sups for restaurants customers to eat food or drink , if much steels are used to manufactured cars product to satisfy car drivers' driving lesiure need , then it may also influence restaurants s' knieves, glass cups price increases, due to cost increase, restaurants need to increase food price to compensate its knief, glass cups price. even, many families feel need to buy many gloass cups to drink water, then it may also influence global glass cups price increase. If one day steel material is shortage , this kind of natural resource must influence restaurants glass cups , knief cost increases. So, their general food price may be influenced to increase. It is not fair to global restaurants food consumers.

Hence, it explains resource shortage may influence some kinds of business cost increases, as well as consumer foods, products services price increases. It means that " resource shortage may influence some kinds of businesses cost increases".

In fact, in our societies, natural resource shortage may influence any kinds of business cost increases, w.g. car manufacturing industry, if one day stell manufacturing material is shortage. it will cause many car manufacturers can not buy enough steels to manufacture cars. When, global car buyers number increases, but global cars number can not increase rapidly, due to steel material can not supply enough. Then, cars prices may be influenced to raise. SO, it seems that steel resource shortage may bring reasonable chance to let global car manufacturers to raise cars prices. When , global car buyes ' new car purchase needs are increasing, hence, natural resource shortage may influence some kinds of business produce prices increase in possible, when the kind of product , such as many people begin to chose to buy new cars, more than second hand cars. The, when steel material supplies shortage, it may influence new car price increases in global can market.It means that any organizations ought not waste natural resource. Otherwise, it may influence their cost increases.

Environmental resource scarcity would likely have been adaptivve in the human evolitionary parst, resources in the environment and organization resource shortage problem might alsoo effect how satisfied they were. Hence, organizations in virtually every industry face the challenge of new managing resources effectively. The influence would run the other way instability as rival, such as big data platforms for e-commerce organizations, e.g. e-book publishers, online sellers. Big data platforms lift limitations on the size of computing resources that can be applied for data, in other words, data storage and e-commerce organizations can significantly influence computing efficiency.

Hence, organizational resources may also influence computer industry information gathering intangible resources, if the electronic books publish, or online electronic commerce product sellers can gather the most up-date consumer individual purchase behavioral data in short time daily rapidly. Then, they collect the most accurate electronic books readers or the kind of online product buyers past purchase choice in order to judge whther which topics of books are the most popular or which kinds of product to the most popular to let them to implement sale strategy, e.g. whether which topic of e-books prices need to be increased ot decreased, whether which kinds of products prices need to be increases or decreased. So, the big data gathering speed is the technology resource to e-commerce market organizations.

Management accounting science how applies to Amazon ecommerce organization

Management accounting concept can help organizations to do management budget strategies, e.g. margin analysis, capital budget, inventory valuation and product cost budget, trend analysis and forecast . Management accounting also called managerial accounting or cost accounting, is the process of analysis business costs and operations to prepare internal financial report, records and managers decision making process in achieving business goals.

However, management accountants depend on standard financial statements containing the earning statement, cash flow statement and balance sheet. In addition , it also makes use of additional finds reports in analysizing the information of the organization including budget performance and cost reports. I shall attempt to explain how management account science can help organizations to analyze cost , why and how changes in order to avoid expense increases or excess cost cases or loss increases.

For Amazon e-commerce publish organization example, Amazon publish is a famous publish organization. It applies internet (online) channel to help authors to sell electronic books and paper books to different countries readers. It also cooperate to other publishers to deliver any its anthors books to their webstores, so when one reader chooses its publish partner webstores to buy Amazon any author books, then Amazon publish will share royalty income between them. Hence, Amazon publish may be book distribution partner to its other e-publish partners.

● How management accounting cocept can help Amazon publish to manage its cost effectively in order to increase its profit or e-books or paper books sale ability.

Amazon publish is a e-comerce organization. It depends high internet speed to help global authors to register Amazon publish's individual author account , then any global authors may download their book files to produce any ebooks and papers to sell from Amazon publisher webstores as wellas global any readers can apply Amazon publish webstores to buy any author individual paper or ebooks from its web-publish stores rapidly. So, Amazon publish must need have fast speed internet technology to support its books sale ability,

It brings this question: How much does Amazon publish internet expenditure need? Does it need to pay shops rent per month? Because Amazon publish has none any actual book shops to locate in any countries. So, Amazon publish must not pay rent to any countries for its shops. Although Amazon publish does not need to pay rent for any book shops, but Amazon publish needs to pay extra internet expenditure to US internet service provider to support its electronic webstores daily electronic books and paper books every purchase transaction, any countries author individual book electronic files download per day 24 hours . So, Amazon publish must need to pay more expenditure for internet service to support its authors and readers their electronic books and paper books purchase and sale transaction per day 24 hours.

As Amazon publish case, in its financial report indicates , it does not pay any book stores rent expenditure or book stores (shops) building building expediture on its profit and loss account, but Amazon publish must need to pay internet service expenditure to US internet service provider. Moreover, this internet service expenditure must be more amount, due to it needs to provide its webstores online book (electronic books and paper books) to sell and electronic library e-book lending service to global readers, 24 hours. Thus, internet service expenditure must be Amazon publish long-term influential transaction expenditure because, any electronic books and paper books, even e-library books borrow service and readers must need to pay visa card for borrowing book month service fee and purchase books from amazon publish e-publish webstores in any time every day.

Hence, Amazon publish must need have good management account strategy in order to predict whether different countries will have how many readers click to its different countries e-publish webstores to spend time to choose different authors books to buy or borrow to read from intenet channel. So, any countries readers budgeting number, readers reading habit behavior, e.g. US has about one million online readers click Amazon e-publish webstores , but it has only three thousands readers pay visa card to buy its ebooks and paper books from its Amazon electronic publish webstores, in this week , but next week, US has about seven thousands online readers click Amazon e-publish webstores, but it has three thousands readers pay visa card to buy its ebooks and paper books. Hence, it seems tha although this week has one million online readers click to Amazon publish electonic webstores to seek any books, but the book buyer number has only three thousands. Otherwise, although next week, it reduces three thousands e-readers click to visit Amazon e-publish webstores e-readers number , but it still keep same three thousand e-readers to choose to buy Amazon publish's books to read.

I assume that Amazon publish needs to pay a fixed internet service expenditure, e.g. US $500,000, but it design this e-publish webstores can help it to do its different countries e-publish webstores, their daily e-readers visiting number, daily electronic book and paper book sale number and daily e-readers visiting time statistics. It's electronic publish webstores can help it to record any countries' reading habits and reading taste , e.g. how many fiction , story books have sold in the week, how many non fiction books have sold in the week , e.g. business topic books have sold next week.

So, Amazon publish can use its e-publish webstores to gather above data in order to make author book topic sale choice, e.g. whether this week, US market ought sell how many consumer psychological topic book, US market ought sell how many management topic book next week. If this week US market can only sell one thousand consumer psychological topic book to compare its budget is less than one thousand consumer psychological topic books budget sale number reduces, e.g. in the week, there are two thousands readers choose to buy consumer psychological topic books from European market in this week. It implies that there are many European readers who like to read consumer behavior books recently. Hence, Amazon can attempt to concentrate on encouraging authors to write more consumer psychological books to let European readers to read within next several months.

Basic on above effects, Amazon needs to provide rapid internet service to European libraries, schools ,e-book partners to help them to promote Amazon consumer psychology topic books in order to let the European consumer psychological students, consumer psychology lecturers, consumer psychologists to know Amazon publish can provide more different topics concern consumer psychology research in order to increase Amazon 's consumer psychology book European market book buyers bumber.

As above case, I assume Amazon publish needs to pay a fixed internet service expenditure , e.g. US$500,000 per month. Amazon needs webstores to evaluate whether it is value, if it helps European schools, libraries organizations to pay internet fee, in order to let they can let many consumer psychology students and teachers and consumer psychologists to know that Amazon publish may have enough different consumer psychology books to be provided to European publish libraries, schools readers to read. For example, I assume next several month, Amazon publish needs to pay US two million internet service expenditure to global different European countries to help Amazon publish itself to promote its al different authors' consumer psychology topic books as well as it evaluates that it will sell different European countries; students , teachers and consumer psychologists readers, they have about three million readers at least choose to buy its one million consumer psychology topic authors; paper books and electronic books next several months as well as it also needs to evaluate whether it can earn more than US ten million at least royalty income after reducing author royalty from all European countries book markets.

Thus, if Amazon publish makes decision to help European countries schools, public libraries to pay internet expenditure to help it to advertise its one million consumer psychology topic authors electronic and paper books to sell. It must needs to pay fixed US$500,000 internet expenditure for Amazon publish its all e-bpublish webstores and it also needs to pay extra two million internet service expenditure for global all European countries libraries and schools per month. If next month, Amazon publish can earn more than US tem million at least royalty income after reducing author royalty from all European countries book market. Then, Amaozn publish ought attempt to make this internet service expenditure for all European schools, libraries organizations, if it had confidence to earn this royalty amount from European consumer psychology book readers, such as this Amazon publish.

On conclusion, , this Amazon publish organization case, it may attempt to apply management accounting science method to make book sale number budget, royalty income budget, even analysis to reader individual reading habit, book topic choices, book sale price evaluation in order to judge whether the kind or topic book ought concentrates on selling to which countries marekts, such as Amazin publish case, it also may choose different consumer psychology topic books to concentrate on selling to different European countries in next several months, if it can earn all European royalty income more than its internet service expenditure to European schools, libraries, then Amazon may attempt to make this decision. Otherwise, it won't be good decision. Hence, it implies that management accounting is one kind of business management science, it can apply number to help any organizations to do right or reasonable reason more accurate as well as it is different to traditional financial acounting, it only helps organizations to record and income and expenditure, earn or loss record function. Hence, management accounting may help any organizations to attempt implement useful or effective strategies in order to improve themselves performance.

How management accounting concept applies to investment

Can we apply management accounting concept to investment decision aspect? An organization's investment decision may make risk, so they need risk evaluation to decide whether the project can bring ehat benefit before they want any decisions. Risk management is the process of assessing, managing and mitigating losses . This applies to both business and investing risk management exists in many forms throughout the financial world, such as one individual investor decides to buy low risk government securities, instead of high yield corporate bonds in an example of risk managment companies and investors frequently use financial managment method like options, and future and strategies, like portfolio and investment diversification, in order to effectively manage risk.

For investment management strategy example, it is professional asset management of various securities, including shareholdings, bonds and other assets, such as real estate, in order to meet specified investment goals for the benefits of investors. Investors may be insurance companies, pension funds, corporations, charities, educational organizations or private invetors.

The term asset management is often used to refer to the management of investment funds. So managerial accounting is the process of identifications, measurement , analysis and interpretation of accounting information that helps business leaders make financial decisions and efficiently manage their day operation . The main objective of managerial accounting is to maximize profit and minimize losses . It is concerned with the presentation of data to predict inconsistencies in finances that help managers make important decisions, such as investment decision for Amazon publish book sale country market choice for which topic of books which are the most popular, in order to concentrate on selling the topic of books to the country market. So, Amazon publish needs to gather past different kinds for any one country, number data may include each author ebook and paper books sale prices, each author different book topic books sale number , in order t make which topic of book sale to which countries investment decision aims to increase readers number t o the country book sale market. So, Amazon publish may be apply these tools of management accounting to gather datas to concern book sale record. They may include: Financial accounting, financial statement analysis, book cost accounting, fund flow analysis , cash flow analysis, standard costing, marginal cost, budgetary control , management accounting tools.

● How to apply mental accouting method to predict investor behavior?

The main aim of management accounting to investment includes planning, controlling and evaluating. Thus, the advatanges to investment may include; better decision making, increase business efficiency, simplify financial statement, raises profitability, motivates employees, cost control, reliability. Hence, management accounting means " mental accouting", it is a concept in the field of behavioral economies. Mental accouting refers to the different values of person places on the same amount of money, based on subjective criteria, often with detrimental results. Mental accouting is a concept in the field of behavioral economies. Developed by economist Richard H, it contends that individuals classify funds differently and therefore are prone to irrational decision making in their spending and investment behavior. It refers to the different values people value on money, based on subjective criteria, that often has detrimental results, mental (managerial)accounting decisions and behave in financially counterproductive or detrimental ways, such as funding a low interest savings account when carrying learge credit card balances, to avoid the mental (managerial) accounting bias, individuals should treat money as perfectly used tools when they allocate among different accounts, be it a budget account (everyday living expenses), a spending account or a wealth account (saving and investment). Also abother author indicates that managerial accounting means mental accounting, which appeared in the Journal of behavioral decision making, the begins with this definition, " mental accounting" is the set of lognitive operations used key individuals and households to organize, evaluate , and keep tracks of financial activities. He considers of how mental accounting leads to irrational spending and investment behavior.

● How mental (managerial) accounting concept helps Amazon publish to make investment decision?
I believe that Amazon publish may apply mental accounting concept to help it to predict whether which topic of books will be the most popular to sell to the country market more accurately. The reason concerns that it can apply all data gathering to analyze whether past has how many readers paid visa to buy the topic of electronic or paper books to prepare to the country , e.g. in this year, Jan. it had 40,000 readers buy fiction electronic books and paper books from Amazon publish US market website to read , it had 100,000 readers buy fiction electronic and paper books to read in European market website and the

year Feb. It had 70,000 readers paper books from Amazon publish US market website, it had 200,000 and paper books from Amazon publish European market website. Now, it is Mar. So, Amazon publish may make assumption that fiction (story) topic book is accepted to read by American and European readers, due to US fiction readers had increased 30,000 number in past one month and European fiction readers had increased 100,000 number in past one month.

However, US and European readers number data is not enough to evaluate whether US and European fiction readers number may still keep to increase. It depends on other factors, e.g. fiction e-book and fiction paper book sale price, if one author's ficton's ebooks and paper books rising prices whether it will influence US and European fiction book buyers make book purchas decision to the author's any fictions. So, Amazon publish need s to make the author's past different kinds of fiction books sale prices record in order to judge whether his fiction book's variable price (changing price) will bring negative or positive impact to his readers' fiction book purchase decision. For exmaple, if the author (A)'s one fiction price increased 10% to ebook and paper book sale price between Jan and Feb. His fiction readers number won't be influenced to reduce, even his fiction readers number can still increase 10%. So, it implies that this author's fiction is attract or popular to US and Eurpopean fiction reader market. Amazon publish ought concentrate on helping this author (A) to advertise his fiction to let many US and European readers to know.Hence, it explains that Amazon publish may attempt to gather past every author individual writing book topic book sale proce whether it is increased or decreased how much %, book sale number in order to make book sale investment decision to concentrate on helping whom to advertise to sell to which book sale country market.

So, it seems that mental accounting concept can be applied to Amazon publish to help it to do any author individual book sale country market advertisement investment decision. For example, if Amazon publish can only spend US$10,000 advertieing expenditure to help author (A) to sell fictions to US and European both markets in Mar. , then it can help author (A) to increase 20% more fiction sale number to US and European both markets. This advertisement expenditure is worth to spend for this author (A) in fiction market.

Hence, it implies that mental accounting concept can be applied to publish investment market, such as choosing which country to sell which topic of books, e.g. US sells more which fiction or European sells more fiction or Japan sells more management business topic books or UK sells more consumer psychology business topic books. All of these issues will be any publisher's important book sale market decision . It may influence their royalty income because if the publisher makes wrong decision to sell not popular topic books to the country market, e.g. in the month, US ought have many business topic readers to choose any business topic books to buy from any publishers, if the publisher makes wrong decision to find many fiction authors to help it to increase fiction stock to prepare to sell to US book market. Then, excess fiction stock may cause low fiction price (fiction book supply or publisher's fiction stock number) is more than fiction book demand (readers). Otherwise, it can not increase business topic books royalty inocme to US book market, because it has not enough different topic, such as management, consumer psychology , accounting, economy , marketing topic business books stock to be putted on book shelves to let US readers to choose when they visit US any book shops in the month.

On conclusion, it explains why mental (managerial) accounting has close relationship to influence customer behavior in behavioral economy view. Mental accounting is a management science or behavioral science tool to help any businessmen to make the most effective or the most reasonable busines decision in nowadays society.

Management science accounting concept how predicts market changing

Accounting aims to help any organizations to record whether the year has what kinds of expenditures, how much of every kind of expenditure finds what factors to cause the kind of expenditure needs to be spent too much in order to avoid excess spending, measurement profict or loss level why what factors cause the year had loss or profit growth in order to achieve long term performance improvement or avoiding loss. Hence, accounting system is not only for bookkeeping record financial performance aim. Accoungint may be one kind management science concept to be applied to explain why and how market changes in order to predict whether the company ought implement which strategies to grow up its business groth or increase clients number.

The question concerns why the organization can apply accounting concpet to predict how the market will change in order to avoid profit falls down or loss causes. I shall attempt to explain as below:

For a watch product sale organization example, this watch sale compay own 100 expensive price watch brand products stock to prepare to sell, their sale prices are between US$3,000 to US$5,000 , so the watch brand prices are below than US$3000, they belong to low prices. It has 100 low price watch brand products stock to prepare to sell. Hence, every month, it keeps exact 100 high price of brand watch products stock and exact 100 low price of brand watch products stoc to prepare to sell. I assume this watch company can sell 100 low price watches and 100 high price watches in this month, but next month, it can sell 50 low price watches and 0 high price watches. Hence, it means that next watch , low prices watches sale number falls 50 number and high price watches sale numbe falls 100 number. It ensures that this company's profit may be influenced to fall by the high and low watch price client reducing number factor. However, this company still lacks data to know whether its competitors ; watch price is the main factor to influence its watch buyers number reduces or whether other factors influence its watch buyers number reduces, e.g. whether its high and low watchs are attractive or not attractive to high its watch design buyers number reduces or whether smart phone product invention influences watch users begin feel watchs have not be importnt to help them, because smart phones have time record function, they can replace traditional watch products or this month has higher unemployment rate, so it causes people do not like spend easily , in special, watch is not one kind essential product. Hence, it seems that this watch company can investigate its every month whether its low and high price watch stock sale record in order to attempt tp find whether what are the main factor to cause its watch sale number increases or decreases? I shall follow above every possible points to be investigated by accounting concept in order to explain why its watch low and high price customer number sudden reduces.

I assume that this watch company's last month and this

month every high and low price watch brand's sale prices are stable. So, it seems that the influential factor won't be its " increasing sale price" to cause its high and low watch price customers number sudden reduces. If it gathered data concerns its watch competitots similar famous watch brands of general price range. It discovered their general sale prices do not have much difference between itself and their famous brnad of watchs. Also, it discovered that their these famous brand high and low price watch sale number is more than its sale number, e.g. the another similar famous watch brand company can sell 200 high price watchs and 200 low price watchs last month and 400 high price watchs and 400 low prcice watch this month. So, it seems that its high and low price of watch is not main factor to influence its watch sale number, because its high and low price watch's their price level had not changeed within these two months . Moreove, its watchs manufacture material costs had not increased within these two months. So, it ensures that its profit falls must not be influenced by watch manufacture cost increasing factor. Hence, it may depends on its accounting record to conclude the main factors influence its high and low price watch sale number reduces, they may include; poor watch design feeling to watch buyers factor, smart phones increasing need factor, unemploymenr rate rising factor.

The next step concerns how this watch company can apply accounting concept to find whether the main factor is poor watch design feeling factor, or smart phones are popular accepted to replace watch product feeling factor, or rising unemployment rate factor which one influences it s high and low price range watch sale number decreases can apply accounting cencept to investigate which is the main factor to influences its watch sale number decreased in this two months? I shall attempt to confirm this possibility as below: Firstly, I assume this watch company's accounting record has marketing promotion expenditure, its expenditure includes advertisement fee, exhibition expense only, however, in its expenditure group accounting record, it has none design expenditure with these two months. Hence, it seems that its high and low price range fanous brands watches had not been improved by its improvement design skill method in order to improve their watch style, picture, shape, colour, function , design to satisfy watch buyers'changing watch fashion need in this competitive market. Hence, it seems that poor watch design feeling factor may be one main factor to influence its watch sale number decreases. It implies that accounting record may help it to find lacking new fashion watch design factor may be one main influential factor to cause watch buyers choose to buy other similar famous brands' watch products.

Next, whether accounting concept can help this firm to judge whether smart phones influences its watch sale number? I assume that smart phone products had been selling more than 10 years in this country in this case indicates US country. So, smart phones mus be its long time similar time seeing function competitors in US. I assume that its past 10 years high and low price range famous brand watches sale number must be more than these two months as well as it had not increases high and low price range of watches prices within this 10 years. Hence, it can depend on its past 10 years accounting record to judge whether smart phones product invention may influence watch buyers number decreases within these two months. basic on its past 10 years , accouniting record indicated that its high and lw price range watch sale number had been increasing, and it s watch price had not beedn increased and its markting advertisement promotion expense had been reducing much within 10 years. Thus, its past watching expense and watch price sale amount and profit accounting record may help it to conclude that smart phone product sale to US market is not the main factor to influence its recent high and low price range watchs sale number falls.

Finally, I shall explain whether this watch company may apply accounting concept to explain whether this month's high unmployment rate factor can influence geeral watch buyers' consumption desire as below:

I assume that this watch company employed 20 watch salespeople and their salaries range are between US$2,000 to US $4,000 per month in the first years . It operated till to this month total 20 years . However, its accounting record indicated that its watch salespeople number had been increasing from 20 to 50 number recently and their salaries range had been increading between US$3,000 to US$6,000 permonth. Hence, within these 10 years , this watch company employees number and their salaries range had been continue increasing. . It may depend on its past 10 years accounting record for salespeople salaries and employee number to reflect whether higher unemployment rate is the main factor to influence its watch sale number reduces.

I assume that within these 10 years, its unemployment rare was between 1% to 10%, in US society , although it may had 1% to 10% young people unemployed within 10 years. But, this watch company, I could also increased salespeople employees number and their salaries could also increase more significantly, even their salaries had not decreased in these 10 years. Hence, its accounting record of salsepeople salaries increasing trend , it may reflect this US watch market's local and overseas watch buyer individual buying watch desires ought not be influenced by slight rising unemployment rate factor, it is based on that this watch company will like to increase salespeople employee number, when it discovered there were many potential watch buyers visited its any watch shops every day within past 10 years. Hence, it implies higher unemployment rare won't influence watch potential buyer individual visiting to any one watch shops in US within these 10 years. So, this watch company's past salespeople salaries, employees number, and their salaries rising range record can reflect whether US higher unemployment ratio level can influence its recent high and low price range of watchs sale number decreases in US local watch sale market.

On conclusion, we can depend this watch company past 10 years accounting record to judge whether which one may be the most main fluential factor to influence its recent watch sale number reduces. I make the final conclusion that its poor watch design feeling factor ought be its main factor to influence its recent watch sale number reduces, due to it had not spend any design expenditure to improve its watch style in order to attract many watch buyers' choices within these 10 years. So, I believe that accounting concept can help any companies to revise whether what factos influence their businessess to be better or worse, instead of general booking record function.

Accounting trademark loyalty theory

In accounting theory view, any organizational goodwill or trademark, they are intangible asset because they can not touch, they are the company name. However, when the organization grows up a long time, ususally more than 10 years, if they are famous when consumers choose to buy the kind of product, they will must remember, then the organization's trademark or goodwill, company names will become the company's intangible asset in their balance sheet , financial report, e.g. Cock Coke soft drink, " Coca Coke" may be this soft drink company's trademaek , intangible asset to this soft drink company. Because any country's soft drinkers, they must remember Coca Coke brand soft drink before they make any brands of soft drink purchase choice. The reason may be Coca Coke soft drink . Its brand had been popular to be accept to be the first soft drink choice to any countries people. Hence, Coca Coke soft drink compnay must put is brand name to be intanginle asset in balance sheet, (B/S),

Why does Coca Coke's brand name (intangible asset) value may increase or decrease in B/S. The reason is simple, when general consumers feel Coca Coka drink has better taste to compare other brands soft drinks. Then, they wil choose other brand soft driks to replace Coca Coke soft drink. So, if the year, Coca Coke's any taste of soft drinks sale number decreases, then it will feel its intangible asset of trademark value is devaluation, but if its soft drink sale number increases in this year. Its intangible asset of trademark value will increase in its B/S.

Hence, it explains why Coca Coke 's trade mark value can reflect its soft drink sale number whether it increases or decreases in the year. Thus, any firms mist hope their trademark , goodwill valuation can often increase every year. The question concerns how they can often keep their trademark valuation to increase? Can the firm increase sale number , it can represent that it has long term goodwill valuation increases? Can other factors influence or impact the firm's goodwill valuation changes? I shall attempt to give examples to explain these questions as below:

In fact, goodwill or trademark represents the company's famility whether how many consumers can remember its brand name , when they choose to buy the kind of product . So, if the firm's products are famous in market, Its products must have many consumers can remember it before they choose to buy the kind of product. So, product's familiar to publish,which ill be one measurement tool to judge whether what may be its goodwill valuation. If there are many consumers remember its brand before they want to buy the kind of products, the firm ought raise its goodwill valuation. It may make market research to enquire whether consumer will choose to buy which brand of product among several similar brands of product. It many people choose to prefer to buy its brand. Then, its brand familiar level to publis will be high grade. It may raise to goodwill valuation inB/S.

So, I think that goodwill fact valuation can not be measured by sale number or sale price or profit or loss amount. It ought be measured by market familiar level. If the product can have many people know its brand exitence in market. Then, its goodwill , intangible asset valuation ought be increased. Otherwise, if there are not may people know or they are familiar its brand existence in market. Then, its probable valuation ought need to decrease . Hence, any firms' goodwill valuation ought reflect their market familiar level for standard.

Do you feel firm goodwill valuation can represent its market value or product sale effort? In accounting principle, goodwill valuation must be measured by money. For example, Coca Coke brand goodwill valuation, in fact, Coca Coke had not pay another in B/S. Its goodwill valuation increases, it is not due to it pays its firm pays cash to buy goodwill. It is due to its capital increase. But, in fact, it does not need to increase cash to capital balance amount in B/S. Because coca Coke has not increase its cash amount, due to goodwill valuation increases. Its goodwill valuation increases, it supposes that is capital amount also be influenced to increase. So, Coca Coke 's goodwill valuation can not represent it has profit growth. Goodwill valuation only represents it has profit growth. Goodwill valuation only represents Coca Coke's present market valuw whether it increases or decreases in soft drink market. It is not actual cash available value. So, why firms need have goodwill valuation. The reason is simple. If one day, the firm hopes to sell its busines to another. When the another potential business buyer feels this firm's goodwill valuation is high. It may persuade b make business purchase decision more easily. because he believes that there are many people are famkliar this product brnad , then they will choose to buy theis product in preference . So, good goodwill valuation can build good business sale image to help the firm can raise business sale price to anyone . Such as Coca Coke soft drink goodwill case, if it can keep high goodwill valuation, then it can persuade any businesses buyers accept to pay high business purchase price. so, B/S goodwill valuation may help any famous business to sell to anyone in the high business sale price more easily.

Can goodwill valuation help the firm to predict market environment changes? For Coca Coke soft drink case example, I assume that it estimated its goodwill valuation is US 3 million , but this year, it estimates its goodwill valuation falls down to US one million. What factors influence Coca Coke feels its goodwill valuation reduces US two million in this year? I believe that is current year goodwill valuatin falls, it has relationship to whole global soft drink taste changes to global soft drinkers. The factors influence global drink makes taste changes , they may include: global soft drinkers begin to dislike to choose to drink any brands of soft drink in preference, if they feel soft drink is one kind of bad health drink. They may choose to buy freash fruits to eat to replace any soft drink. I assume that the other soft drink brand companies' goodwill valuations are decrased. It means that if other soft drink brands' goodwill valuation can increase. Then, Coca Coke may believe that there are many soft drinkers prefer to choose other soft drink brands' soft drinks to drink. So, global soft drink markets still have competitive effort. Coco Coke nees to learn how to change its taste and let soft drinkers believe its soft drink can bring health to them to compare other soft drink brands. So, it seems that goodwill valuation also helps any organizations to eveluate how market changes to influence itself product sale effort. It explains why goodwill valuation is one kind of good market changing predictable tool t any businesses in accpunting concept, instead of sale business valuation measurement tool.

On conclusion, accounting principle or accounintg concept is not only be applied to bookkeeping financial record aspect. If the organization hopes to find what factors to influence its customer number or they hope to predict whether market will ought how to change to be netter or worse. It may attempt to investigate its past every year some kinds of expenditure amount record in order to find how any why the firm itself needed to pay more or less to the kind of expenditure. It aims to research what factors may influence its past and present expenditur changes in order to find whether what the most influential factors are influenced itself buyers number increases or decreases .

Hence, accounting is one kind of makret research scientific method to any organizations.

Accounting science how predicts e-commerce consumer behavior

Cash e-commerce organizations apply accounting record to predict consumer behaviors? If it is true, how e-commerce organizations can use past accounting record to predict consumer behaviors? In general, e-commerce sale transactions must need any individual e-buyers to register higher address to their e-store in order to deliver products to any one-buyer homes. For Amazon e-commerce organization, when one China client buys a furniture from US Amazon e-commerce organization, when one China client buys a furniture from US Amazon e-store. The furniture is putted to Amazon US itself warehouse. So, when the China e-buyer pays visa to buy the furniture . He needs to register his address to amazon e-store. When amazon confirms that it can receive cash from the China e-buyer visa card, then amazon will deliver the furniture from US amazon warehouse to the China e-buyer home by plane.

So, amazon must have any e-buyer address record and the product sale price record for any one country e-buyer after it comfirms that the e-buye visa card has enough money to buy the product. Thus, amazon can apply past every online transaction to follow these data to do market research, they may include: which country person buys the product, what the product is, how much to the product price, how many of different product number e-buyer purchase within the year. So, amazon can collect all above data to analyze any one country has the highest e-buyer number,e.g. in the year, there ar one million US e-buyers number, there are two million China e-buyer number,which kind of products are the most popular, e.g. soap , computer, furniture, cloth, shoe, shirt, towel, electronic products etc. what the age range is, e.g. young , old, students , workpeople, they choose to buy the kind of product, how many number , the family buys the kind of product to the e-transaction, how many goods return number to the year total e-transaction, how many goods return number to the year total e-transactions. Hence, amazon can gather all past every e-transaction data to prepare how to predict whether how every country e-transaction will consumer behavior to predict whether how every country e-transaction will influence consumer behavior will change next year in order to let it to prepare how to implement new market strategy,e.g. how to advertise its product, which countries need to spend more advertise to promote its products, evaluate whether amazon needs to spend how much advertisement expenditure to earn more e-sale transactions number to the targe sale country.

Why does amazon's any one e-transaction's accounting record assists it to predict consumer behavior? For china target e-buyers market example, when one Shanghai city e-buyer pays visa to buy one computer from amazon e-store, if the e-transaction can be accepted . Amazon can gather the e-buyer is living in China Shanghai city, which brand of computer , he chooses to buy, how much sale price to the computer, how many of computers number , he buys, how many e-transaction times to the China, Shanghai city buyer within the year. Hence, when amazon needs know where China target market has how many e-buyers number to every city, how many e-transaction return goods and refind number, which kinds of product are the popular to China e-buyers' purchase needs, which is the highest price and the lowest price sale level to China, Shanghai city target e-commerce market every e-transaction . Thus, when amazon collestc all above China, Shanghai past one year any individual e-transaction data, it can compare whether how its China, Shanghai city.

Nest year, e-buyers behavior change in order to analyze whether which kinds of product price ought need to reduce in order to attract many China e-buyers to click amazn webstores to pay visa to buy its products or which kinds of product price may increase, when the kind of product is popular to sell to China target market, or make out of e-stock shelf decision to the kind of product when Amazon discovers the kind of product is not accepted to buy in popular from its e-store. Thus, it seems that Amazon's past any one e-transaction accountning record can help it to analyze whether how every target market its e-buyer behavior is changing in order to change next year sale changing strategy is more reasonable . Hence, it explains why e-commerce organization's accounting record may help it to analyze how future market changes as well as record how every old e-buyer customer whether he/she will choose to buy the kind of old product again or buy new product, even not buy anything from Amazon e-stores this year.

Hence, any e-commerce organization's e-stores can apply online technology skil and accounting concept to help it to learn how to analyze every year post efficient countries' cities different e-buyer individual product behavioral choice in order to judge/revise whether it ought need to change to buy its products from its e-stores conveniently. So, any e-commerce organization explains why it can attempr to apply its post every accounting e-buyer sale transaction record to make every country consumer behavior marketing analysis to compare transaction visiting shop business model more easily, because visiting shop sale model can let the seller to sell its products in its shop, when it locates in the country. But e-commerce sale model can let the product can be sold to different countries more easily.

So, it seems that if the e-commerce organization can have good accounting record system to keep its past all e-transactions record can gather all data concerns any countries e-buyer individual address , how much sale price for the product, how many sold, and refund to the country e-buyers and the e-buyer age is young or old , male or female e-buyer purchase habit.

Can the e-commerce organizatin predict consumer behavior if it implemented inefficiency accounting record system? Firstly, we need to know good or right accounting record system can help the organization to track or find past any transactions more easily. So, if the organization has none good accounting record system , its accounting record system can not be improved efficiently. Then, its accounting record may bring wrong sale price record, wrong profit (over -profit) or less profit or wrong loss (over loss) number record. Then, this wrong sale transaction record may mislead financial performance to publis to know, e.g. current year, its sale performance is improved, but in fact, its current year sale number is less than last year sale number. Consequently, this organization can not predict its consumer behavior. Whether know to change exactly, due to it often has wrong sale number record, e.g. higher or lesser sale price record, and more or less sale number may influence its gross profit earns high amount, even if its any kinds of expense record is more orless, it will influence its net profit is more or less or less is more or less, for example, if the organization earns US one million dollar prodict this year, but due to it smore sale number transaction to cause over profit. So, its financial performance report indicated its earned US two million dollar. So, it believes its buyers number can increase, if its sale prices do not change. This wrong financial performance report many mislead it has good consumer behavior in this year. Then, it will continue implement its old marketing strategy. Consequently, its next year financial performance may be caused worse to compare present. So, it implies that wrong financial record may cause wrong consumer behavior judgement.

Can robots perform management accounting analysis tasks

Our future will experience artificial intelligent development stage. Nowadays, we had had some tasks which can be done by robots, e.g. warehouse delivery, restaurnt kitechen dish cleaning tasks, transport tasks, even non drive manual auto driving tasks, shopping center service etc. cleaning or customer service simple jobs duties. If one day, robots cab be applied to do office tasks, e.g. accounting record tasks, they may replace account clersk, even accountants to deal simple accounting record tasks, even complicate management account analysis tasks in office working environment. If future robots can be developed to help accounts clerks as well as accountants to do simple bookkeeping debit and credit every income ot expense transaction record in order to analyze marketing research tasks, then it brings this question: Can future robots replace accounts clerks and accountants to do their accounting tasks in any organizations. I shall attempt to research the relationship between robots and accounting tasks questions as well as whether robots will bring what social influence if robots can replace future human to do any simple and complex accounting tasks for any organizations.

What is need for development of artificial intelligence to accounting tasks aspect? The first computer language used to create artificial intelligence is USP. This language is quite flexible and extensive . Features such rapid prototyping and macro are very useful in creating AI. LISP is a language that makes complex tasks simple. So it seems that it is possible tobots can learn human to do any kinds of accounting tasks, e.g. financial account record, audit check, management account analysis etc. different kinds of acounting tasks for financial , management account, audit check functions in any organizations.

However, scientists believe that artificial intelligence can help accountants be more productive and efficient. Robotic process automation RPA) allows machines or AI workers to complete repetitive, time-consuming tasks in business processed, such as document analysis, handling that are plentiful in accounting . AI can also significantly reduce financial fraud and maintenance accounting errors. Hence, the stages of AI development to accoutning industry, they may include: internet AI, business AI, perception AI, and autonomous AI ., Internet AI is thr simplest stage of AI, business AI has a limted memory, perception AI. This is the first stage in the future of AI. A key feature of this perceptive form of AI is the ability to compile and draw from past experiences, much like human to accounting tasks.

The design phase is essentially in literative process comprising all the steps releveant to building the AI or machine learning model, data acquisition, exploration, management and analsis tasks. So, it seems that future robots may be developed to help human to do simple and complex accounting tasks. Combining AI with other technologies, such as robotic, process automation can follow accountants to redirect the time that they used to spend on multiple tasks, toward performing high-value, high -impact taaks. Adding AI to accounting operation can also increase output quality by miniizing human errors. So, AI and automation won't be replacing finance and accounting professionals in the foreseeable futue.

On the contrary, as AI automates many aspects of business, there is a bug opportunity for accounting and finance professsionals to upskill themselves to meet the requirements of the 21 centurey. For AI audit task aspect, AI enables the analysis of a full populatin of data and can identify outliers or expectations. By making it possible for auditors to work better and smarter. AI will help them to optimize their time, enabling them to use their human judgement to analyze a boarder and deeper set of data and documents.

Can AI be used in auditing and accounting ? In the assurance practice, AI is being used to perform auditing and accounting prcedures, such as review of general ledgers, tax compiance, preparing workpapers, data analytic, expense compliance, fraud accounting skills. So, it seems that future AI can replace market research analysists, compensation and benefits managers , instead of financial accountants, management accountants an auditors in any organizations.For bookkeeping clerks position example, these simple account jobs are expected to decrease, by 8% 2024, and it's non surprise because most bookkeeping is getting automated if it has not been as of now, Quickbook, Peachtrss etc. accounting software that does not need any more, because robots do not need any kinds of accounting software to help them to do any simple or complex accounting tasks.

How has teachnology changed the accounting industry? Computers and accounting softeare has changed the industry complexity, with but when robots develop, it will change global accountancy professional more complex. Can robots replace accountants? Automation had brought significant changes the accounting profession over the last decaed. When some tools have made accountants lives easier. However, since robots invention, it developed these tools have also created a false debate about whether automation will overtake the global accounting industry compexity and make accountants irrelvant . The question should not be whether automation will take over accounting, but where its rreal value lives.

In fact, I believe that no any software can match the critical thinkning and trusted counsel that a human advisor offes, as valued accountants, have become business partners, where software is limited to evaluating concrete inputs, accountants can understand clients business goals and observations voice to make decisions. This allows them to serve as advisors to their clients, whether by adjusting business models in real time, or managing emplyer wellbeing . Sok, future AI development ought not replace human accountant's this kind of skill more easily.

● How robotic process automation impact on accouting industry changes?

Searching for methods to efficiently perform accounting tasks can be dated book to the 1950 s, when process mechanisation involved the use of punched cards to store and retrieve transaction data (Keenoy, 1958). Since then IT ad automation have transtormed the way accountants collect, store, process and share data through a variety of tools (Ellis, 1986); Kaye, Nicholson, 1992; Rom, Rohde, 2007). However, robotis process automation is a technology solution that allows end-users to comfigure a software robot to use existing applications to perform accounting transactions manipulate data and communcation with other systems (introduction to robotis, 2015).

Software robots can be easily programmed or trained to perform repetitive, rules-based , high volume operations by replicating human actions when accessing multiple systems, applications, and documents (Embracing robotic automation 2018). Hence, robotic accounting software can bring cost reduction to counting and finance tasks, e.g. one robotic accounting software can replace two to five full time accounting clerks, increased process speed, software robots perform routine tasks faster than employees would manage mamually (Cacity, Willcocks, 2016) . They do not get distracted or tried and thus avoid delays, cycle times decreases significantly improved process control and performance visibility, e.g the collected analytical information is much more detailed and can be used for audit and compliance checks, higher quality data (accuracy, consistency, compliance), e.g. robots can validate the data before reporting or using them future. Assuming that the appropriate rules have been thoroughly tested beforehand, data inaccuracy and quality risk decrease fill tracking and logging robots' action make internal and external audits easier and reduce compliance risks, continuous operation 24 hours a day, or none working day limits. So, robots are applied on accounting task aspect, it can bring positive impact on employees, repetive tasks taken over by robots release employees' times. They can shift their focus on higher value added tasks, solve employee morale proble,. Any accounting department staffs may feel tired when they need over time works, often but robotic accounting staff won't have tired or bored feeling.

However, robotic process, automatin may be applied on these accounting tasks aspect, they may include: internal control period end clising, general ledger, subledgers, closing , validatin of journal entries, low-risk accounts, reconsiliation, consolidation, reporting-monthly , quarterly close, internal performance and management reportng aggregating and analysing financial and operational data, external statutary report, accounts receivable and payable record-maintaining updating customer/supplier data, creating processing, posting payment, collections, billing, matching invoices, aganist sales and purchase orders, cash management, general accoutning, inter-company transactions, inventory accountancye, travel and expenses reimbursement request, audit and document expense report, payroll, stock keeping, fixed asset accouting record, tax accounting. So, the general simple accounting tasks robots will have effort to finish.

● Can robots perform the same management accounting analytical decision making skills to human management accountants tasks?

Although, robots can perform simple bookkeeping audit accounting tasks, but whether complex management accounting analytical and decision making tasks, robots can do the same level of management accounting analytical, decision making tasks to human management accountants?

I shall attempt to answer this question. How robots impact of mental accounting in valuation? No retailers show this price without considering the " 99" in end. This indicates to our mind that the price is cheaper. Its popularity can be verified gas stations all around the world. The difference between robots mental accounting issue and management accountants.

The Anchoring theory was used to verify its possible impacts on capital venture tech finds decisions, during equity trading for an initial investment starting. Management accountants ususally arrange 68% of the finds use-valuation as a basic, when 21% proposed other methods . But still use valuation and only 11% of the investors said they did not consider valuation at allo. the context considered that the human management accountant will consider that the investment would be made in a startup in early stages. That is with little or any real accounting information can image the amount of uncertainty that exists in the type of analysis?

Moreover, why do even experienced fund managers invest based on an impossible calculation> In simplity, it explains that human management accountant in order to do any investment decision. Although robotis will use alaytic mind more than calculating to estimate any investment risk in order to make investment decsion for any organizations. AI's analytic skill and human management accountant calculation risk skill be their difference on how dealing management accounting investment risk issue aspect. Even, the difference between human management accountant and robotic management accounting automation is their robotic management automation can apply mental accounting theory to judge consumer behavioral choice.

It is a new model of consumer behavior is developed using a hyrod of psychology and microeconomics. The deveopment of the model starts with the mental coding of combinations of risks and losses using the prospect theory value finction. Then, robotic management accounting automatin can attempt to evaluate of consumer purchase for the product is modeled using the new concept of " transaction utility", e.g. one family electronic firm, it is seeling rice cooker, television radio, household electronic products, it can learn how to mental accounting method to help this houseold electronic product firm to predict how any why its different kinds of household electronic products choice may change to its consumer behavior next week, e.g. robots can gather wlectronic product competitors prices data to compare itself company's same kinds of electronic product data e.g. rice cooker prices and its competitors' rice cookers prices, whether its high price , rice cookers price factor or other factors influence its rice cookers sale number decreases in this week. Consequently robotic management accounting software may help this household elecronic product company to analyze whether what are the actual factors to influence its rice cookers prces reduce in this week. It is human management accountants feel difficult to collect past price data in order to make accurate consumer behavior changes, prediction or find whther are the main factors to influence product sale number increases or decreases.

Hence, future robotic management accounting automation can learn the valuation of purchase modeled using the new concept of transactin utulitym such as this houseold electronic product case, robotic management accounting automation many learn the household budget process ,the characterization of mental accounting, in order to find whether household purchase behavior to the company's products whether what the main factors may influence its household producys sale number increases or decreased.

On conclusion, future robots can do simple bookkeeping, audit check , general daily accounting tasks, even robots can also do complex management accounting tasks, they can learn how to apply mental accounting knowledge to gather the company's past all every month different price variable data, sale number, in order to conclude whether what are the main factors to influence the kind of product sale number increases or decreased more accurately to compare human management accountants in any organizations.

Applying HR management accounting learns consumer behavior

Managerial accounting purposes to be used by management in "making by business decision: It includes product caost, budget , forecast and various financial analysis consumer behavior is the series of behaving of patterns that consumers follow before making a purchase through consumer behavior, you can also earn how customers interact with and the year products. So, any organizations may attempt to find any management account past year past per month transaction records to bring consumer behavioral change predictiver knowledge, it can help future decisions about product creation more easily.

Hence , the management accoutning knowledge focuses the process of creating organization goals by identifying, measuring, analyzing, interpreting and communicating informations to managers is call management or manerical accounting. Management accounting focuses on all accounting aimed at informing management about operational business metics. Also, any managers may attempt to gather past product number presentation date to find whether what the main factors can influence consumer buying behavioral change in its any kinds of products, the level of motivation also affects the buying behavior of customers, e.g. whether the products' sale prices sight rise, to influence customer number reduces, or whether the product's traditional old design is not more attractive or popular to accept to compare other linds of competitors' similar product design, or whether the kind of product is not popular to be accpeted to use, the another how invention of similar product ot the market is recession , it need to change another new sale market, if replaces its existence etc. different factors.

Hence, management accounting can help managers to attempt to gather past the product's sale and production past data to carry on analyzing whether what the main factor to influence its customer number reduces or increases in other to improve its sale strategy.

● Computer sale applies management accounting to predict consumer behavior

For computer sale product example, the computer saller may attempt to apply management accounting to analyze why computer buyer behavioral changes, e.g. a study of consumer behavior will reveal what kind of consumers buy computers, could they buy for home and personal use or for office, what features , they look for, what benefit o they seek including post purchase service, huw much they are willing to pay how many they are likely to buy . All of these computer buyer individual purchase behavioral analysis, the computer seller can follow its different models of laptops, desttops, prices, sale number, house or office ise design kind etc. data to research and analyze and predict hether future computer buyer individual need will how changes, in order to prepare and learn how to design new kinds of desktops and laptops to raise competitve effort.

In fact, in computer industry, the factors may influence computer buyer behavioral change, they may include core technical features, past purchase services, price and payment, conditions, physical appearanre, value added features and connectivity and ability are the main seven factors that are influencing consumers' laptop purchases choices.

● How can the laptop computer seller applies management accounting data to analyze whether which is the main factor to influence laptop buyer behavior changes?

for last month, I assume that laptop model (A) laptop computer sale price si per US$1000 and it can sold 1000 number and laptop model (B) laptop computer sale price is per US$1,500 and it can sold 2000 number.SO, it implies that although laptop model (B) computer sale price is more than US$500 to compare laptop model (A) computer, but the model (B) laptop computer can still sell more than 1000 number fo compare model (A) laptop computer last moth. It seems that model (B) laptop's attractive dsign, more fuction, rapid connectivity and mobility and attrative physical appearance main factors may influence laptop (B) model computer products sale number is more than laptop (A) model computer products last month. But, in this month, it has significant change between laptop model (A) and laptop (B). In this month, laptop modle (A) and laptop model (B) prices are not changes, but laptop model (A) can sell 3,000 number and laptop model (B) can sell only 500 number. Consequently, their sale numbers have significantly changes, laptop (A) can increase more 2,000 sale number, but laptop model (B) can decrease 1,500 sale number between these two months. It explains that although it seems that laptop (B) model has possible own attractive physical appearance, and rapid connectivity and mobility, more function to cause it can sell more than laptop (A) model computer produc. But, it ensures that all of anh one these possible factors can not help it to raise sale number in long time. It means that laptop model (B) may have other factors to influence itss sale number, e.g. other brand of laptop computers' physical appearance, more function, connectivity and mobility , features , even they can provide better value added sale service, repair service, product delivery service, feature to compare this brand of laptop seller, or its laptop model (B) buyers had lost confidence to use its laptop model () computer products, because they often need to repair and pay extra repair service fee frequently, e.g. one year has one time to two times at least per year. SO, their past poor frequent repair experience influences they choose to buy other brand of laptops. Otherwise, why laptop model (A) computer products number can sell more 2,000 number , the factor may include non rising price, none frequent past repair experiences to any one model (A) laptop buyer , their individual psychological positive feeling factor . So, it seems that gather these two laptop model (A) and model (B) past sale number, sale price data to conclude whther what main factors may influence its model (A) and model (B) laptop sale number to increase or decrease in long term.

However, this laptop computer seller can not only depend on the gathering these two months short time sale numbers ans sale prices data to model (A) and (B) laptops, in order to make the final conclusion concerns whether what the main factor can influence model (A) and model (B) laptop product sale number changes absolutely. It must need to continue to keep the long time management sale umber and sale prie data record for laptop (A) and (B) in order to conclude whether what the most accurate influential factor is that it can influence laptop model (A) and B() sale number both change in order to implement the improvement strategy for them both.

● Management accounting data can also help this laptop seller to predict future market development or whether which market will have high sale effort, e.g. Japan laptop sale market may have the highest market share ratio, among different Asia countries, or Germany laptop sale market may have highest market share ratio among different European countries next year. For example, in the last year, this laptop computer seller had sold 50,000 laptops to Japan computer market, it has sold 500,000 laptops to China computer market, it has sold 100,000 laptops to US computer market and 50,000 laptops to Germany computer market, in this year. its these laptop markets sale prices are not changed, it has sold 200,000 laptops to japan computer market, it has sold 400,000 laptops to China computer market, it had sold 200,000 laptops to US computer market and 200,000 laptops to Germany computer market . Hence, it ensures that Germany laptop market has increased 4 times sale number from last year and Japan has increased 4 times sale number from last year. Otherwisem China laptop sale number has decreased 100,000 laptops from last year and US laptop sale number has increased 1 time from last year. So, it can imply that Germany and Japan future laptop sale number may grown rapidly to compare US and CHina laptop sale markets. It also indicates this sale trend also may help this laptop computer to attempt to find whether what factors may influence its US and China laptop sale number fells down,e.g. whether this local laptop choices increasing factor, it laptop physical appearance is not more attraction, or slow connectivity and mobility speed ,even their model (A) and () laptop prices are higher to compare US and China local other similar brands of laptops prices.

In summary, I believe that management accounting technique can be attempted to apply to help any kinds of products to find whether what main factor(S) to influence their product sale number changes, it is one kind of good data gathering and analytical tool to help any businesses to attempt to predict consumer behavioral changes.

Organization management accounting strategy

What is organization management accounting strategy? As its most basic an organization management accounting strategy is a plan that specifies how your business will allocate resources, e.g. money, labour, and inventory to suppoty production, marketing, inventory and other business activities. IN general, the foure organizational straategy and the culture of the organization categorized into four types: Adhocracy, market and hierarchy.

The purpose of an organization management accounting strategy can be defined as the direction an organization takes with the aim of achieving future business success. Strategy sets out how an organization intends to employ its resources, including the skills and knowledge of its people as well as financial and material assets, in order to achieve its mission or overall targets. So, the key element of an organizational strategy may include: define vision, create mission, set objectives, develop strategy, outline approach, get down to tactics. However, an organizatinal strategy plan is an organizational management activity that is used to set priorities, focus energy and resources, strengthen operations, ensure that employees and other stakeholders are working toward common goals established agreement crowd intended outcomes/ results, and access organizational missions.

Adhocracy strategy is a form of business management accounting that emphasizes individual initiative and self organization in order to accomplish tasks. This is in contrast to bureaucracy which relies on a set of defined rules and set hierarchy in accomplishing organizational goals. The term was popularized by Alvin Toffler in the 1970s. Examples of adhocracy include most project or marix organizations. Among private-sector organizations, high technology firms, particularly young firms facing fierce competition are sometimes organized as adhocracies. However, important examples of adhocracy do exist in government. Hence, adhocracy is a flexible, adoptable and informal form of organization that is defined by a lack of formal structure that employs specialized multidisciplinary trams grouped by functions. Adhocracy is characterized by an adoptive , creative and flexible behavior based on non-performance. Adhocray culture in a business context, is a corpoate culture based on the ability to adapt quickly to changing conditions. Adhocracies ar characterized by flexibility, employee empowerment and an emphasis on individual initiative.

The five basic marketing strategies may include: product, price and promotion and people in management accounting strategy aspect. They are key marketing elements used to position a business strategically. A market strategy refers to a business's overall game plan for reaching prospective consumers and turning them into customers of their products and services. For example, the

BSC business 2 customed marketing strategies may include : social networks and viral marekting, paid media advertising, internet marketing, email marketing, direct selling, point-of-purchase marketing, co-branding, cause marketing, conversational marketing. Hence, marketing strategy or management accounting strategy is a long term toeard looing approach and an overall game plan of any organization or any business with the foundemental goal of achieving a competitive advantage by understanding the needs and wants of customers.

Hierarchy strategy describes a relations of corporate strategy and sub-strategies hierarchically and logically consistent at the level of vision, mission, goals, and metrics , e.g. HR strategy (human resource strategy), to general, the three levels of strategy are: corporate level strategy, this level answers the foundamental question of what you want to achieve, business unit level strategy focuses on how you've going to grow.

The management accounting strategy planning hierarchy is the organization's mission and vision both of ,which should be long-lasting and motivating. At the base of the hierarchy are the shorter term strategies and tactics that unit members will use to achieve the vision. So, the basic levels of management accounting strategy are: corporate, business, functional and operational level strategy. The strategic hierarchy aims to be concept used to understand the different types of strategy decision made in a organization, e.g. michael porter , three generic strategies (cost leadership, differentation, and focus) that can be implemnted at any organizations. So, hierarchical levels of strategy managment accounting may be concerned with selection of which is the right generic strategy to implement, sale method, such as low product sale price, lot differentiation of product choice, and focus an main product feature market sale methods etc.

● The relationship between organizational management accounting strategy and avoiding resource waste

If an organization can implement good managment accounting strategy whether it can assist it to reduce any organizational internal resource waste, e.g. exceed human resource employment cost, facility used cost, using cost, efficient administration or management cost etc. essential organizational cost. Because any organizations must need to use resources in order to achieve efficient providivities, service activities, if the organization can implement effective strategy in order to measure its performance, whether strategy can assist it to judge how to avoid not essential resources spending. Can efficient strategy help organizations to avoid to waste resources? I shall attempt to explain as below:

Whether formal strategy implement can avoid formal technical measurement of scale and concentrates on the loca resource mobilization using aspect os small, medium and large organization? What does resource mobilization strategy mean? Resource mobilization refers to all activities involved in sesuring new and additional resources for your organization. It also involves making better use of and maximizing , existing resources.What are the stepd in resource mobilization?

Firstly, any organizations need to plan od designing a resource moilization strategy and action plan, secondary , finding key elements of a resource mobilization strategy, thirdly,act of practical step to implementatin, fourth identify, fifth step, engagement, sixth step, negotiate, eventh step, manage and report, final step, communicating results.

What are the source of resource mobilization to any organizations? For example includes spreading flyers, holding community meetings, and recruiting volunteers. Material may include financial and physical capital, like office space, money, equipment, and supplies . Human resources, such as labour experience, skills and expertise in a certain field.

How does an entrepreneur mobilize resources? To exploit opportunities, entrepreneurs monilize and recombine a variety of resources, such as financial capital (e.g. cash, ot loan from a bank , human capital e.g. skills from a employees, and social capital e.g. information obtained from social contracts. Hence, the overall objectives of the resource mobilization strategy is to securce the necessary funds to deliver on the source mobilization strategic outcomes. To achieve this accurate resource used number and expenditure budget and emergency appeals will need sufficient preditable and contrributions. So, the aim of resource mobilization strategy outlines how secretariat will organize the process of prioritising, plannin, selecting projects, monitoring: broadening the resource channels, as well as coordinating with staffs for mobilising and effectively utilizing resources.

So, the genesis of resource mobilization strategy is a good, solid strategic plan, it should articulate activities that are more routine in nature and can be finded through the organizational internal efficient resource mobilization. Resource mobilization refers to all activities involves in securing . These new directions or new business opportunities are pursued using a distinct resource mobilization strategy .

On conclusion , an efficient resource mobilization plan is a term resource mobilization, it refers to all activities undertaken by an organizations to secure new and additional financial, human and material resources to advance its mission. Inherent in efforts to mobilize resources is the drive for organizational sustainability . So, resource mobilization is about an organization getting the resources that are needed to be able to do the work it has planned. Resource mobilization is more that just fundraising, it is about getting a range or resources from a wide range of resource providers for donors, through a number of different mechanisms. How does an entrepreneur mobile resources? To exploit opportunities, entreprensurs mobilize and combine a variety of resources, such as financial captial , e.g. cash or loans from a bank, human capital e.g. skill from an employee and social capital e.g. information obtained from social contract.

Why do organizations need resource mobilization strategy? The reasons may include: The principles of resource mobilization wih examples, it focuses on forging partnerships built on trust and mutual accountability . So, as to attract adequate and more predictable contributions, with the future goal of sustainability, it refers to all undertaken by an organizatin to secure new and additional financial , human and material resource to advance its mission, in efforts to mobilize resources is the drive for organizational sustainability, community mobilization is the process of bring together as many stakeholders as possible to raise people's awareness of and demand for a particular programme to assist in the delivery of resources and services, and to strengthen community participation for sustainability an dself -reliance, resource mobilization is often referrred t as " new business creaating chance" , the organization has a strong, yet flexible structure , such as writing proposal how to spend the least respurce expenditure in order to achieve the most satisfactory effective result to the organization.

Hence, developing a resource mobilization strategy plan , as the source of new business opportunities to the social and behavioral change considerations must be needed the organization as well as resource mobilization target at a minimum level should be needed to raise at transformational change happen on the ground and advocate for the products and may have to develop new business proposal.

● Can resource mobilization change improve organizational performance?

I believe that resource mobilization can help any organizations to change or improve performance to the better, even the best. I shall explain as below:

What are the sources of organizational change? Change originates in either the external or internal environments of the organization. External sources include political, social, technological or economic environment, externally motivated change may involve government action, technology development, competition , social values and economic variables.

How do organizational resources affect change? Results indicate that organizations possessing greater stocks of historically valuable resources were much less likely to engage in adaptive strategic change, but also that this resoure-driven towards change tended to have a even beneficial effect on performance . Wonder of organizational change management is easier spoken about than achieved by resource mobilization strategic in possible? Can create enterprise level value by effective process for resource allocation?

The key to success involves managing organizational change , so it leads to real and lasting improvements, tailoring to resource allocation how mobilization strategy. So, nowadays, organizational capacty for change: Increasing change capacity and avoiding change overload, organization, today risk is overcommitting resources, resulting in an overload condition wih which it how allocates its resources to tbe used efficiently or inefficiently. For example, on new government regulations, ne products development or growth aspect, organizational change efforts often run into some form of human resistance. First, management staffed its human resource departments with spend most of that time in efficiency. So, whether how organizational change is better, it depends on how it changes its old resources, e.g. human resource, facility, equipment resources, even management time resources to change new improvement resources change to be better . It means providing the resources, budget, authority, credibility and commitment for the effort to truly organizational change on improvement.

● Why does organizational resource budget need?

For example, managing a human resource department involves budget planning and execution . The human resources budger refers to the finds that how HR allocates to all HR processes. Unit should include in an HR budget. It may include: number of employees, projected for next year, benefits cost increases or decreases, salary cost increases or decreases, projected turnover rate, calculation, actual cost incured in the current year, new employee welfare benefits. programs planned, other changes in policy, business strategy , it may impact costs on HR cost aspect. So, an organization needs to budget whether it will have how much on what kinds of resources spending aspect, including human resources, facility, equipment and water , electricity etc. natural resource , it budget is a tool used for planning and controlling financial resources. It is a guideline for future plan of action, espressed in financial terms within a set of period time, knowing organization's priorities, objectives and goals helps it prepare organization resource budget.

Effectively leveraging people and budget, resource management is critical for organizations to ensure . They are optimizing and allocating resources to the right initiations, e.g. from a human resource perspective, the data needed to create a new budget include the following number of employees, working arrangement tasks time, management time, employee salary cost, due to costs that only impact the human resource department and impacts the entire organization both aspects. So, efficient HR cost budget can help refine goals that reflect realistic resources and how memebers of the organization to use fund because employee retirement can be expensive and it can b increased or decreased expense in any time, when the month needs increase or decrease employees number to any departments. It depends on whether tasks rate is needed to increase or decrease. So, an organization's HR cost budget can help how it makes the most accurate HR resource expenditure.

Organizational facility, equipment, shop, office, warehouse space resource budget why is important. Office space is as an enabling resource, equipment and furniture to enhance the organization's ability to achieve efficient operations and activities of the best organizational performance. In view of this analysis, facility planning personal would be one important factor to influence whether the organizatin can spend the least expenditure to use its resource. During business growth, any facility equipment, office , shop, warehouse space must increase , moreover staff puts increasing number on existing resources, so be sure to budget in order to make another option is to least equipment instead of buying it, whether you need moving insurance for important equipment and machinery, set budget to help prevent overspending.

All of the tasks that are include in maintaining a facility, such as equipment maintenance and building facilities whether are needed to improve, facility oversight, warehouse and special equipment whether is qpproriate space for customer service and uses resource dynamic of an organization's work patterns with work. It depends partly on the resources an organization is willing to invest or not, when it feels this facility resources are very important to influence its performance.

● What does organization office , shop , warehouse space resource management strategy?

Organization and using space must be land resource, if the organization can manage how to use its space in efficiency, then it can improve service performance or productive efficiency. Space management can be defined as a practice where an organization manages its physical space invnetory which includes tracking , control, supervision and utilization, planning of the space available. So, space management is the mangement of an organization's physical space inventory. Ths involves the tracking of how much space an organization has managing occupancy information and creating spatial plans. So, one efficient space resource using organization, it needs to undertake annual property assessment reviews, leverage individual projects to drive portfolio evoluation applya planning methodology on all project rises, utilize planning to define direction and scope focus on mathematics before graphics, define and collect only the required data on warehouse, shops, office, buildind space using aspect. For example, a space management ffice can give the organizatin an accurate picture of how many employees , it needs to have space for an average day, and show it the trends of demand for this space across weeks and months. This can help the organization to determine how many permanent desks could be converted to hot desks in office, warehouse or shop , saving space. For example, space managementin retail aspect, it is the process of managing the floor space adequately to facilitate the customers and to increase the sale.

Shop space management is very crucial in retail as the sales volume and gross profitability depends on the amount of space used to generate those sales. Space management is a multi-step process that requires data gathering, analysis , forecast and strategizing. In prective, it involes creating a space management system that occupants throughout your organization, so whether the organization realizes it or not, every organization needs to know how to manage its space one way or another , if it hopes to improve its service or productive performance. Make use of these strategic space management and planning techniques, efficient and an unplanned, unmanaged office is not likely to magically transofrm into a well organized of productivity. So, space management is the management of an organization's physical space inventoty , employee working environment, shop product putting sheleves locatin, equipment, desk putting location. All of this tangible space physical factor may influence overall organizational service and/or productive performance and /or sale performance. So, space may be an organization's land usng resource because any organization's land using space must be limited size, they must have land space using shortage challenge if their products stock number increases, but warehouse space can not increase or shop products shelves number can not increase, but product sale number increases.

● The relationship netween organization behavior and resource using management accounting

Has organizational behavior and resource spending, they have close cause and effect direct relationship ? When one organization can perform better, whether it represents that it must spend much resource to use or when it perform poor, it represents that it must not spend much resource to use. Organizational behavior is a field of study that investigates the impact that organizational psychology and human resource management, the cause and effect relationship.

How organizational behavior effects an oganization? Organizational behaviors propose that inventives are motivational factors that are crucial for employees to perform well. It changes the way people make decisions, e.g. decision to increase or decrease resources to use, when the organization feels that it has resource shortage or excess. However, businesse that are able to encourage risks in decision making within the company culture can enhance innovation and creativity.

In fact, organizational behavior has four main elements, people, structure, technology and external environment. So , tangible and intangable resources may influence organization behavior when it is needed to change by management, e.g. human behavior in a work environmen and determines its impacts on job structure, performance, communication, motivation, leadership etc. for example, when the manager has less time to prepare how to organize this meeting process to his client. His short managing meeting plan time , intangible time resource, it can influence his business proposal to be either accepted or rejected to this client. So , time resource whether it is enough or not. It can influence this manager's client proposal meeting whether it is accepted or rejected in possible.

Every employee behavior can determine the importance of group departments in business productivity. So, it seems that resources whether they are enough , they can impact on employee's performance. As a result, managers are able to maintain better relation with their employees by effective utilization of human resource. So, cause and effect relationship plays an important rolw in how an individual is likely to behave in a enough tangible and intangible resource provided or not enough organization.

Modern organizational behavior is characterised by the acceptance of a human resource model, e.g. whether the plant can provide enough productive equipment facility and space shelf for product putting location in order to raise or improve logistic transport efficiency in warehouse. So, plant warehouse space management and shelf putting location productive equipment facility these tangible resource factors may influence warehouse productive performance. It seems that tangible resource provision amount and space management or intangible resource time management resource, they have close relationship to influence organizational behavior. Consequently, it can achieve the result either performance improvement or worse performance. So, resource and performance organizations , they ought have cause and effect relationship in resource management mobilization strategy view.

● How applying artificial intelligent management accounting solution accounting challenges

One of the biggest challenges for management accountants nowadays is the preparation to face globalization in local and global market. Globalization competition is changing government regulation and innovation in technology had to change in the market environment which have greater impact to an organization. The role of managemet accounting to AI, it may help managers to make any management strategy decision, e.g. evaluate sale price is the most reasonable, sale market choice, customer age target evaluation etc. within any organizations. Also known of cost accunting, management account of the process of identifying, analyzing and communicating information to managers to help to achieve business goals. However, the most important job of management accountant is t condoct a relevant cost analysis to determine the existing expenses and give suggestion for the future activities and make better management accounting, when management accountants need to learn how to apply these management accounting data: financial planning, financial statement analysis, cost accounting, find flow and cash flow analysis, standard , marginal cost and budgetary control, they can be made by AI.

In general, the job dutures of management accountant may include: generate sale among client accounts, operates as the point of contact for assigned customers, develops and maintains long term relationships with accounts, makes sure clients receives requested produsts ans services in a timely fashion . So, they need to learn these different management accounting technique: margin analys, capital budget, inventory valuation and product cost, tend analysis and forecasting. Future AI may be taught to learn all of these any one management accounting technique to assist organizations to make more reasonable management account strategy implementation.

The basic principles of management accounting include communication presents insight which is crucial , irrelevance information is valuable, the influence one value is estimated, credibility,recognizing the requirement, good accounting manager, they need to learn how conflict, be open to new ideas: In management accounting tehnology apply, there are three elements of management control system to develop to future Artificial intelligent management accounting technology delegated decison authority , performance evaluation and measurement systems and compensation, reward system.

Hence, accounting technology in AI development has always played a past in making the accountant's job just a played a part in making the accountant's job just a easier. Its own knowledge of technology increased to have the accountant's ability to analyze statistical values. Technology advancements have enhanced the accountant's ability to interpret data efficiently and effectively.

● Future AI management accountant may help human to the honest accounting record

However, any one managment accountant needs have good professional personal quality, honestly and integrity play vital roles in accounting because they allow investors to trust the information they receive about companies in which they invest. Honesty in accounting is the primary characteristics of the profession that allows financial decision-makers to make appropriate judgement . So, the main focus of management accounting is to assist the management of a company in efficiency performing its function-planning, organizaing, divesting and controlling . Management accounting helps with these functions in the following ways: provides data, it serves to a vital source of data for planning, for product costing method example, it is used to cost methods available are process costing, job and different production and decision making. for 3 types of controls may include: internal controls are typically procedures or technical safe guards that are implemented to prevent problems and protect organizations' assets. Future AI technology may help an organizations to do above all management accounting decision jobs ,even replace human in offices to avoid losses. The traditional management accounting technique includes" the use of performance measures, three ROI , budget systems for planning and control, divisional profit reports and cost-profit volume relationship, and breakeven analysis for decisions. The management accounting reports may include order information report, project report, competitor analysis. They are either internally aor outsourced. All of these management accounting methods, future AI can replace human accountants to do .

● Can AI be applied to help organizations to implement management account strategies ?

The two widely used types of accounting are: Financial and management accoutning, for the strategic cost management techniques example, it is the cost management techniques that aims at reducing cost , when strengthening the position of the business. It is a process of combining the decision making structure with the cost information in order to do the strategy as a whole . Hence the role of management account in the organization is to support competitive decision making by collecting, processing and communicating information that helps management plan, control and evaluating business processes and company strategy . So, the strategy management accounting can be defined as the process of identifying, collecting , selecting and analyzing accounting data . So, future AI can be applied to assist accounting teams in strategic decision making and organization effectiveness assessment must be defined.

Future AI can be applied to these management accounting aspect: For methods and techniques of costing management , it may include: Job costing, advestment, salepeople,bonus, contract cost, long periods of time job, batch cost, process cost, one operation (unit or output) , cost service or operating costing, farm cost, multiple cooperation unit. The tools of cost analysis, breakeven analysis, budget cost control marginal cost analysis, cost control , minimum price analysis, standard cost development , target cost. All of these management strategies, AI can do .

The various tools and technique of marginal costing may include: contribution, profit volume ratio, contribution : sale value , p/v ratio, features of profit volume , break even point . Hence, the AI tools can control cost monitoring in execution. For that AI can help organizations to make cost control budget, it is defined as a AI tool that is used by the management of an organization in regulating and controlling of a manufacturing organization. AI can also perform cost budget for material to any manufacturing organizations to help them to reduce the manufacturing cost , e.g. making material choice for the cheapest price.

AI can gather the product material price, e.g. standard cost and normal cost. Then , AI can help the manufacturing organization to choose the best quality of the cheapest material in order to compare whether which kinds of material to produce the kind of product can bring the high economic benefit to let consumers get more satisfactory feeling. Thus, it is future management accounting development direction for AI.

FIVE

THE RELATIONSHIP BETWEEN RESOURCE SHORTAGE AND CONSUMER BEHAVIOR

Can resource shortage influence consumer behavior changes?

Can bring either positive or negative or both impact to change consumer behavior when the consumer begins to feel resource shrtage occurrence to choose to buy the kind of product or consume the kind of service?

Consumer researchers have suggedsted that chronic

resource scaraity, specially, an inproveished early home environment with fewer resources and high levels of instability and uncertainty can lead to chronic differences in choice behavior (Griskevicius et al. 2011). How are consumers affected by scarcity? Scarcity affects producers because they have to make a choice on how to best ise their limited resources. It also affects consumers because they have to make a choice on what services or goods to chooce. Hence, resource shortage may be situational factor influence, situational influences are external circumstances or conditions existing when a consumer makes a purchase decision. Because the kind of product is facing resource shortage issue to influence the product manufacturer can not have enough resource to manufacture the kind og product. SO, number supply is decreasing, such as cars product, if steel number supply is decreasing, it can influence global car manufacture number decreases. When global new car buyers feel that they can not buy any kinds fo new cars easily. Then, even global new car price rises, they won't influence new car buyers purchase desires. So, in new car sale market, if steel supply number reduces, global new car buyer number will not decrease easily.

How does a consumer make choice with scarce resources? Like producers, consumers also have to make choices, since consumer resources , such as time, attention, and money are limited. They must choose how to best allocate them by making tradeoff. The concept of trade-offs due to scarcity is formalized by concept of opportunity cost. In fact, research in marketing often begins with two assumptions, by scarcity of products and/or a scarcity of resources, dfferent types of scarcity individually and jointly influence.

Consumer behavior , an integrative analysis of research

finding remains that scarcity principle in consumer behavior, it refers that scarcity to the condition of resources shortages, it can affect consumer behavior. So, consumer behavior and resource shortage, they seem have close cause and effect relationship between them. For buying behavior example, when one male consumer with high shopping motivations, when he knows a scarcity arrtibute and thus are a vary limited resources, e.g. he allows to buy the product within 5 minutes , when the shop will close soon and thus a very shop time clising time limited. It can persuade the male customer to make purchase decisin immediately. So, it seems that intangible resource , such as shop closing limited time, scarcity may also be a fundamental phenomenon that influences consumer behavior, when the consumer feels that shop will close, it does not allow himw to continue to stay long time in the shop. The shop closing time nay persuade the customer to buy the product immediately.

It explains that why the influence of quantity scarcity and time restriction on consumer, this implies that when consumers' cognitive resources are not restricted by external environmental factor influence, such as shop soon closing time or web traffic to media, when the online buyer , he dislikes to spend long time to click on any website stores to choose themselves brands of the kind of product choice to make purchase decision. The online buyer may only click one website store to make purchase decision immediately.

So, it explains why online sellers can sell their products firm online stores easily, because their website stores web traffic is not busy at the moment. There are not many online buyers click themselves webiste stores at the moment. So, when there are many online buyers can click themselves webstores to choose any kinds of products in shor ttime rapidly. Then, their online sale chance may be influenced by " not busy website stores web traffic jam to media time factor".

Hence, it seems that when one consumer feels resource shortage, it may persuade the consumer to choose to buy the kind of product immediately. I suggest that people may not only differ in terms of how they choose to consume, this could include encouraging consumers , such as impact pf resource scarcity on price-quality judgement. It means that the predictable " panic shopping" in response, experiencing resource scarcity can also increase a sense of community by encouraging consumer to share shopping experience. So, product uncertainity , which is able to motivate behaviors, such as urgency to buy.

This, scarcity , also is known as paucity, is an eonomics term used to refer to a gap between the buyer purchase desire and external environmental factor, for exmaple time and money are characteristically scarce resources, to urge consumers to make purchases or else they won't guarantee next day purchase the product.

Howveer, the cost of using a resource is called the opportunity cost, the value of the next scarcity in economics connotes not that something is nearly impossible to finf. In common, consumers must choose between correct consumption and future consumption, for example, the COVID 19 crisisi may bring positive urgent time to save product, e.g. medical mouth cover protection product, when many medical mouth cover protection product buyers believe the brand of covid 19 medical moth cover protection products supply is shortage, they believe they ought buy the brand of medical mouth cover protection product supply is shortage, they believe thay ought buy the brand of medical mouth cover protection products immediately.

Otherwise, they can not find this kind of covid 19 medical mouth cover protection products to buy later. So, the anticipation to the covid 19 crisis will help some brands of medical mouth cover protection proucts, they can be sold rapidly . So, panic buying may be encouraged when the covid19 mouth cover protection product buyers feel a common brand share covid 19 mouth cover protection products shortage resource through a collection action. Hence, even the brand of covid 19 medical mouth cover protection products prices are raised, the covid 19 mouth cover buyers still choose to buy the brand of covid 19 mouth cover protection products, because they believe that they can not buy the brand of covid 19 medical mouth protection cover products later, when this brand of covid 19 medical mouth cover manufacturers won't continue to manufacture this kind of covid 19 medical mouth cover products again.

So, it explains that crisis and product sale time limited intangible resources can influence consumers to make a lot purchase decision suddenly. On conclusion, resource scarcity is essentially about current brand for a resource exceeding available supply. Resource scarcity occurs when demand for a natural resource is greater than the available supply leading to a decline in the stock of available resources.

However, limited time may be one kind of intangible resource shortage to influence consumers to choose to make the purchase decision to avoid that they lose the final purchase chance. So, the intangible limited time psychological factor may help businessmen to sell their products in short time, when the consumers feel that they have no enough time to choose any kinds of product to buy or they believe that they can not buy the kind of product later. So, resource shortage may bring position impact to influence consumer behavior in behavioral economy view.

Do they have relationship between organizational resource economic behavior and social needs?

In organizational behavioral economy view, economic systems that shape behaviors and constrain access to resource necessary to organizations and society both. People are influenced to organizations as employees, consumers. IN behavioral economy view, economics is the social science that examines how individuals, businesses and overall societies manage scarce resources. Because none resource exist in unlimited quantities, even internet technology resource , societies must establish priorities and decide how best to allocate resources in such a way that meets as many needs and wants as possible . So, organizational behavioral and economics to explain why employees sometimes make irrational business decisions , and why and how the organization employee individual behavior does not follow the predictions of economic models . Because any organizational employees are emotional and easily distracted brings , they make decisions that are not in their self interest when they are working in organization. Hence, how whether it is more or less any organizations use themselves resource. It may influence the social whether it has much or less resources to society. It can use which interact within the organization, Why have they interaction to influence resource supply between orgaizations and societies?

In sociology, a social organization is a pattern of relationship between and among individuals and social groups. Characteristics of social organization can include qualities, such as division of labour, communication system, leadership , structure of a organization. For hospital example, it is one social organization, whether how it uses its resource , it can inluence whether society has how much resources can use. Hospital is one social resource organization (division of labour), e.g. doctors, nurses teams, cleaner teams, patient customer enquire teams, counter service teams. They are a major influence on social behavior and is the link between human nature reaching to the hospital organizational and social environment. Hoe many actual patients number , social need in the year, if the year , there are not many patients need to feel to go to hospital , then it can influence the hospital feels resource excess, or it won't need to use more hospital resource to serve its patients in the year. S, social patients needs and hospital medicine supply needs, they have close relationship every year. It means that the hospital's medicine manufacture material won't need much, it the year has not many patients or patients number is decreasing. So, shopital organzation hoe to need its resource, it has close relationship to patients number in society (nature, demographic, economic, cultural and social behavior patterns and consciousness). So, it explains why the social organization is the best of all organized human society, such as hospital organization example, its patients number will influence medicine resource need.

Another example is bus public transport service social passengers number choice to catching bus transport tool, it can influence whether how buses use oil nature resources needs. If the year , there are less passengers to choose to catch buses, they choose to catch trams, trains, ferries in preference, then due to every bus reduces passengers numer, it does not often driven , following the fixed timetable. If the bus stations often have no many passengers are waiting buses, then many buses are often staying in bus stations. Consequently, bus oil fuel nature resources need must reduce. Thus, social bus passengers number may have indirect relationship to influence buses oil fuel natural resources needs every year. It means that bus oil fuel nature resource use amount is influened by social passengers public transport tool choice needs. It is one good example bus public transport service organization seems to be one social organization.

SIX

ECOMMERCE ORGANIZATION RESOURCE MANAGEMENT STRATEGY

Why does in this e-commerce organization situation, online webstore speed must be the most important factor to influence its sale success. Information technology internet speed, online webstore design, online transation convenience transaction feeling (tangibale and intangible both resource factors) may influence its future clients number ?

In behavioral economic view, any organizations must need to use resources to carry on any business or working activities. Resources may include: management time to managements, working time to employees, information technology etc. office computer to administration, factory equipment to plant workers, plant or warehouse land space to logistic delivery or goods shelves, electricity, gas , water to workplace , even, employees number. HR to any department tasks. So, it seems that before any organization can finish any activities, they must need enough resources supply in order to satisfy any activities need. If the organization overall itself , even overall society. I shall explain as below:

For ecommerce organizatin example, any online trading firms must need to own high speed internet information technology resource to supply to any one technologic staff store to pay visa to buy any product in the most short time rapidly. So, its online store website speeds must need to be very fast in order to avoid to delay any country clients to carry on online transaction. If the ecommerce business organization can not support efficient, high speed internet service to let any countries online buyers to satisfy its online webstore purchase service. Then, any countries' online buyers may choose another online store to replace to buy its similar product easily.

Hence, convenient webstore online purchase service much be very important to influence this online webstore organization. It seems that technologic online internet resource must be the most influential factor to influence this online websore organization clients number. If its online website store can not supply rapid online purchase speed to let any one country to buy its products from its webstores rapidly. Then, its clients number may be influenced to reduce. So, in this e-commerce organization situation, online webstore speed must be the most important factor to influence its sale success. Information technology internet speed, online webstore design, online transation convenience transaction feeling (tangibale and intangible both resource factors) may influence its future clients number . So, judging whether the kind of resource is the most important to influence the organization's success, it depends on whether it needs to use what kind of resource to carry on its daily activities.

In fact, one organizational change has relationship to whether its reponses can have enough supply as well as its behavior can be influenced by the resources variable , the scarcity of any kinds of resources are supplied to be used. So, I believe that whether any kinds of resources are scarcity in the organizational environment, how much they are used, these any kind of resources can bring relationship to influence how organizational perceptions, interpretations and responses.

How an ecommerce organization resource affects society? Why has online webstore's information technology resource close relationship t influence online buyers number and social job chance?

Organizational impact to the effect on an organization has any reponses to influence how on society chance. However, organizations can also have a positive impact on the economic satisfaction of a town. More oe less jobs supply to the wociety, which can be influenced by whether the organization can have effort to buy how much resources to be used in order to carry on itself any business activities. Hence, it seems that if the organization, such as the above online website sale product organization, if it can have enough money to employ web design professional to help it to design attractive website stores to let attract online buyer purchase choice, as well as paid higher internet service fee to improve its fee to improve its online internet speed in order to let any countries online customers can still click its website rapidly, even in busy online click time. Many people click computer mouse to enter ecommerce website stores in the same time. Then, any one won't choose another websites stores to replace its online sale service easily. Even, if it can buy many advanced computers to let its staffs can use the best quality computers to follow any client's ourchase transaction in short time. When , they confirm that whether the client's visa card payment can accept and what product he has paid to buy from its webstore. Then, the staff can know where the accurate address of the country , the client's product can be delivered rapidly. It will avoid to delay any product delivery. So, if this online store seller can have enough internet information technology source to support its whole computer information department staffs to wrk efficiently. Then, it can increase more online transaction chance in success. Consequently, it can grow up its online sale business, it will create many new potisition, due to its computer information technology department must need to increase employees to help it to deal any countries online buyers online purchase service transactions and online product sale delivery service immediately in order to avoid online product delivery service to global online buyers. So, it can bring more job chance if this online webstore organization can have enough effort to buy high technological computer information products to let its online customer service staffs to use in order to improve online product delivery service store to let global many online buyers' attention . Consequently, it can apply online webstore purchase channel to apply website purchase channel to persuade many global online buyers online purchase choice to its webstore easily. So, it seems that this online webstore's information technology resource has close relationship t influence online buyers number and social job chance.

How do organizational resources affect organizational change?

IN general, resoults indicate that organizations possessing greater stocks of historically valuable resources were much less likely to engage in adaptive strategic change, but also that this resource-driven disinclination towards change tended to have a begin or even beneficial effect on performance . So, in general, if one organization lacks any one of these three important resources. It can influence this organization's performance to worse, they many include: human resource , financial resource, phycial resources and information resource. However, managers are responsible to acquiring and managing the resources to accomplish goals. If the organization can have enough resources to be used. It can bring positive impact to influence its overall organizational performance, even, when it has not any resource scarcity, it can avoid negative impacts on the society, such as increasing jobs chance. Hence, scarcity of capital, human and social resources to be provided to the organization, it will influence the organizational structure changes, even employee individual work attitude is influenced to change worse, when he/she can not have the best resources to be used in order to raise efficiency or improve performance more easily.

How to build organizatonal resource using right psychology

The psychology of management is the branch of psychology studying mental features of the person and its behavior in the course of planning, organization management and the control of joint activity. The human factor is considered as the central point in the psychology of management as its essence and a core. Hence , organizational psychology plays a very important rolw at the time or recruitment very important role at the time of recruitment taking disciplinary action or resolving disputes between employees. HR focus and expertise mainly lies in dealing with people . So , it makes sense that the study of the human mind, how to use organizational resources efficiently.

The organizational side of pschology is more focused on understanding how organizations affect individual behavior, organizational structures , social norms, management styles and role expectations are factors that can influence how people behave within organizations. In general, industrial organizational psychologists use psychological principles and research methods to solve problems in the workplace and improve the quality of life (e.g. avoiding often waste industrial resources in manufacturing process aims). They study workplace workplace productivity and management and employee working styles. They get a feel for the morale and personality of a company or organization, e.g. suggesting to use skills and knowledge relating to psychology how to reduce same productivity level, but the organizational resources can be reduced to use. It is one kind the most efficiency resources using method to any kind of organizations.

On conclusion, industrial and organizational psychologists will often use science to study human behavior organizations and the workplaces. Their aims to help organizations to reduce excess resource using in any manufacturing process in order to reduce cost. Employers who need to attempt to learn how employees use resources to do work activities, it can bring these advanaages : learning how to use neuroscience to attract the right talent, retain high performing employees, because any organizations' resources will be used in order to manufacture any products or work activites by any employees in any time.

Employees are the ones who get the job done. They know how the organization and especially ho w their specigif team works best. So any one employee may be the important factor to influence the amount of resource use, any organizational resource use amount, it has close relationship to any employee work behavior. Moreover, resources, that is , group-level resources associated with shared relationship that foster a quality exchange of information and interaction between individuals within the workplace , helping any one employee to learn more about on the job training, use employee training optios to ensure department leader optimizes the employees' motiviation and potential retention. Aim to give opinions to employees to know how to avoid resource using waste method to achieve cost saving aim to the organization.

SEVEN

OUTSOURCING SERVICE RESOURCE AVOID WASTE STRATEGY

Information Technology Outsourcing

In any organization information technology department, information system operations remain the predominant function outsourced, other functions are also being performed by external service providers and the relationship is between outsourcing and certain demographics: size, industry is formation intensity. The results suggest that system operations remain being performed by external service providers. Further, industry and information intensity has some influence on the extent of outsourcing of certain functions.

The first reason is cost reduction, trying to remain competitive and up-to-date is becoming a financial burden to many organizations. This is true particularly in fields, such as banking and financial services, health care and manufacturing. Hiring outsiders to handle part or even all of its information system often helps an organization to provide better services and maintain a competitive advantage. The information technology industry choice of outsourcing factor is related to size, industry type and information technology.

The second reason is technological and/or human resources in the management of the information technology infrastructure skill improvement. The information technology department outsourcing service to external service provider, includes the degree of internalization of technological resources and the degree of internalization of human resources. Some economists defined internalization of outsourcing service is as ownership is by the focal organization which takes on full control with profit and loss responsibility. Also who define outsourcing is as involving a significant use of resources, either technological and/or human resources, external to the organizational hierarchy in the management of the information technology infrastructure. So the information technology external service providers includes: applications development and maintenance, systems operations, networks/telecommunications management and user computing support, system planning and management purchase of application software, but excludes business consulting services, after-sale vendor services and the lease of telephone lines etc. outsourcing services.

The third reason is economics of scale in areas of hardware, software. This pressure is seen as the most significant factor driving today's corporate interest. An outsourcing service provision might be in a position to exploit economics of scale in areas of hardware, software and staff since it pools different kind of technological projects from many service receivers. Outsourcing information technological service can reduce the corporate's cost with the high level of IT investment, there are increasing pressures to move away from fixed expenditure, corporate overhead towards a more direct variable cost approach to control the IT operations. The IT costs can become predictable for overruns is often placed on the service provider. Outsourcing service can allow the service to gain immediate access to competitiveness in delivering products or services as well as to avoid of obsolescence risk, due to the changes in the nature of the IT infrastructure, the risk of obsolescence is high. Outsourcing can allow the service provider has the ability to diversify these risks across a broad range of service receivers. However, long term contracts might in spread the risk, the weakness is back to the receiver.

It seems outsourcing IT service has also these disadvantages: such as, loss of flexibility or managerial control. Outsourcing reduces real or perceived control over both quality real or perceived control over both the quality of software and the timetable of project since the work is now being carried out by people not under direct supervision. It also threats to long term career prospects to information system professionals because many of them do not find suitable. Is jobs or promising career paths in both areas of the corporation. Outsourcing also increases coordination cost. It may requires increasing time to communicate and coordinate with the service provider. Traditionally, the formal meeting cost of negotiating and monitoring the outsourcing contract are potentially wide ranging, indirect and substantial increasing, such as, additional releasing or transferring employees, in license transfer by software vendors and in re-negotiating contracts costs. So, the IT industry of profit motivates service provider might not be in the least interests of the outsourcing service receivers. Some IT service providers are in the business of maximizing their profit at any cost, this could run counter to a service receiver's interest.

●

Outsourcing or insourcing in human resource supply chain factor

To choosing of outsourcing or insourcing in human resource supply chain factor of the controlling service demanders needs to concern this issues: Should human resource activities be provided in house or should all or past of those activities be outsourced? The relationship between organizational structure and the HR function is an important variable. The individual activities that comprise HR systems include not only the employee life cycle from recruiting to termination, but also planning for organizational staffing needs and improving organizational effectiveness. How organizations need to outsource HR function to not care employees knowledge and skill is a factor to influence any organizations choose to outsourcing non core employees when which have no any right employees to be promoted to do the position. For example, firms engage in HR outsourcing to reduce management access HR expertise, achieve workforce flexibility, focus managerial resources and keep up with changing workplace negotiations. Also, supporting the tend is the availability of common technology platform, which can reduce costs for organizations and risks. However, organizations are afraid of losing some control over delivery of outsourcing services and finding themselves dependent on the vendor or liable for the vendors actions where there are both benefits and challenges may be informed by the structure of the relationship between client firms and these organizations offering the outsourced activities to client firms.

What variables are impacted by HR outsourcing of staffing? Which include: administrative costs for labor expense, client firm to HR relations, HR regulatory competency requirement, knowledge of cost factors, e.g. billing and pay rates, vendor markups and margins, vendor management competency requirement, client and vendor relationship, communication is between client managers and staffing vendor, employee data-available, data quality control, data security, match with job requirement, employee quality, inter-vendor competition, mining of client talent by vendor , quality content for preferred staffing vendor, standardization of business process (intra-company), strategic focus of client firm, demands on client managers vendor competency and external economic environmental viability.

However, it has dynamic relationship between the client firms and staffing vendors. Moreover, the models of human resource supply chain, every has different set of advantages and disadvantages for the client firms. The models can be relate to the decision making process on outsourcing of human resources. As strategic services tactic decisions have an important impact or selecting the particular HR outsourcing model that a client firm adopter. The another model is the balance of power and control over managing the control workers differ to decide what every worker individual skills or abilities outsourcing demand. Moreover, local contracting is also the predominant traditional model for outsourcing staffing with non-core employees. A client firm usually uses several staffing vendors to meet temporary staffing needs for seasonal functions, employee absences and special projects. The advantages of local contracting are high touch and high quality of service by staffing vendors, minimal bureaucracy, empowerment of hiring any high qualified employees to get the job done, and a relatively better fit between specific staffing vendors and functional needs.

The disadvantages of local contracting can increase costs from non-standardization of hiring practices and procedures across the client form, a significant amount of word of mouth and subjective quality issues, high local costs and client firm us subjected to the capabilities of the staffing vendors and contract employees. However, local HR contracting is the most flexible, high quality, but expense, inefficient and ineffective HR outsourcing model for the client firm. Another model is the working period to be decided to outsource HR contracting. In this situation, in the short term and on a day-to-day basis, the client firm aims to achieve on economy of scale with its staffing vendors. The total costs of temporary workers as well as internal costs for contracting with several different vendors are higher than if it needs one staffing vendors to meet all its needs. So, the client company can set the reasonable pricing that it pays for its temporary outsourcing staffs. Each staffing vendor secures a different rate range with each vendor as opposed as one contact. In the long term, it is benefiting, each specialized staffing vendor is able to fully work with each function needs temporary utilization is better than the average. Mismatches are fewer. Functional departments are able to receive a high quality / high touch service in any time period. Another model is the centralizing is when the department standardizes the staffing process to drive costs down of temporary workers. This tends to occur when a percentage of non-core employees reach a certain ratio of core employees. The advantages include more uniform standards in hiring process, billing rates and pay rates, departmental hiring managers can refocus their effort to choose outsourcing staffing, criteria may be established for a performed suppliers list and greater security for the staffing established vendors that offer higher quality services. The disadvantages include new departmental responsibilities in HR which decreases outsourcing efficiencies for the organizations daily administrative direction is rather than long term strategic direction. Usually lacking qualifications to fulfill the responsibilities, overall, centralizing of HR outsourcing is that firms can achieve more standardization which additional bureaucratic costs and the necessary non-core jobs do not get done as a need. Another model is purchasing HR, which manages staffing vendors from HR to the purchasing unit of an organizations. The goal is to continue cost reductions by increasing efficiencies. In conclusion, the main benefits of HR outsourcing include maintaining organizational control over the hiring process, application of purchasing capabilities for greater standardization in hiring processes pay rates and bill rates. So, any outsoucred HR organizations may be reduce hiring process cost.

●

Global outsourcing source strategy
in a value supply chain

What is global outsourcing source strategy in a departmental role? In a highly competitive global environment, many manufacturers are responded by setting and outsourcing relations for components and finished products with lower cost producers on a contractual electronic commerce department, (original equipment manufacturer basis). Outsourcing strategy is part of the value supply chain of corporate activated. Nowadays, global outsourcing increases organizational and technological capacity of firms and cooperating a network of remotely located external suppliers performing. These understanding the important roles that product designers, engineers and production managers and purchasing manager etc. play in global sourcing strategy empowerment. Specially, electronic commerce is popular to supply chain. For example, Toyota car manufacturing company, owns unique capabilities by designing and manufacturing certain car components in-house , i.e. insourcing. Toyota also outsource manufacturing activities, Toyota adopts purchasing necessary, but no strategic inputs from independent component suppliers on obtaining a lower cost for these inputs. For example, products would be belts, tires and batteries to vehicle products that are not customized and do not differentiate its products from its competitors. Toyota's outsourcing strategy is car strategic inputs provide differentiation, e.g. engine, transmission etc. are sources from suppliers based on strategic partnership to gain to access to suppliers' capabilities and it is also a conceptualize global outsourcing sourcing strategy to Toyota car manufacturing company.

How value chain outsourcing affects firm level performance. Global outsourcing strategy means to identify which production units that will serve which particular markets and how components will be supplied for production and thus included a number of basic choices, companies can make in decision how to serve various markets. Either choice relates to the use of inputs, assembly or production within the country to serve a foreign market or decides to use of internal or external supplies of components or finished products. In this outsourcing source input situation, the term sourcing is needed to describe how multi-national companies mange in of components and finished products in serving foreign and domestic markets. Sourcing decision making is both contractual point of view, the sourcing of major components and products are occurred by multi-national companies. First is from parents or their foreign subsidiaries. Second is from independent suppliers on a contractual basis. The first type of sourcing is known as insourcing. Otherwise, the second type of sourcing is referred to outsourcing. How to achieve economies of scale by outsourcing or insourcing sourcing input strategy? Therefore, the two outsourcing strategies are multi-faceted and require careful examination.

●

Outsourcing benefits in economic view

The two economists (Abrahamson & Rosenkopf, 1993) indicated that In long term, outsourcing can help to reduce fixed investment in finance view point, in-house manufacturing facilities and thus lower the breakeven point, which subsequently helps boost an outsourcing company whose return on equity (ROE). Thus, if any one corporate performance is evaluated on the basis of its contribution to the company's ROE. Also, in the short term or long term on resource inputs outsourcing view, early adopters of outsourcing strategy indeed experienced efficiency gains as they were able to reduce fixed investment in in-house manufacturing facilities and lows their ROE. But, later adopters may have different to gain institutions legitimacy or because of competition pressures in the industry, despite some inherent uncertainties about the long term costs and benefits of outsourcing strategy. It seems that outsourcing strategy was devised as any organization's policy makers to access trade linkages of benefits for short term or long term. Outsourcing strategy is a systematic analysis of the economic, political and regulatory implications indicates potential benefits along with a number of potentially negative side effects to any organizations. Then, outsourcing strategy will be caused this question: How to assess the risks and benefits of outsourcing for organizational sectors and nations both? The decision to change outsourcing behavior to carry a business activity may have profound implications for outsourcer and outsource receiver both, but little impact of the sector level. The common occurrence of industry decisions to outsource most manufacturing, including sale of factories, it created a new sub-sector, contract manufacturing. Otherwise, at a national level and public sectors become less distinct to outsourcing strategy. Public policy on outsourcing has stimulated extensive debate, privatization social justice and value for money etc. challenges.

●

What motivate outsourcing what is being outsourced risk and concerns?

Whether what motivate outsourcing, evidence of what is being outsourced risk and concerns? Outsourcing activities include: outsources manufacturing components and other value adding activities. Some focused on employment is outsourced another firm's employees carrying out tasks previously performed one's own employees. Outsourcing is an activity outside the organization's chosen core competencies. It seems outsourcing is a sub-contracting relationships between firms, all foreign production, hiring of workers in non-traditional jobs, such as control workers and temporary and part time workers.

What are the motivations for outsourcing reasons? Why outsourcing is needed to any organization. For example, it can enable firms to focus on core activities. The concept of focus originates in operation on a small, manageable, number of tasks at which the operation becomes excellent to specific technologies and as a risk of vertical integration advantages. Other benefits of outsourcing appear is literature on strategic management, operations management, purchasing and supply and innovations.

Moreover, outsourcing can improve flexibility to meet changing business conditions, demands for products, services and technologies by creating smaller and more flexible clear evidence includes improved creditability image, greater workforce flexibility and avoiding being backed into specific assets and technologies are harder to measure. How outsourcing can improve company performance. For airline manufacturing industry example, Hill & Jones (1995) showed that the manufacture of a large portion of the Boeing 767 is Boeing's third largest commercial aircraft, which is outsourced to Japanese manufacturers, which include Fuji, Kawasaki and Mitsubish. As a result, only 10% of the value of the 767 Boeing is produced in-house. So, outsourcing is an attempt to enhance manufacturing air place industry competitiveness.

●

How can choose smarter outsourcing?

How can choose smarter outsourcing? Organizations hope to do sight options to save money, among themselves staff layoffs and a reduction of overhead costs, such as office space. Private companies have long outsourced in order to save time and money. During periods of economic growth, many organizations began to use outsourcing more frequently and staff workloads grew in proportion to increase budgets. Tasks such as conducting needs assessments, reviewing proposals, conducting site visits, monitoring and creating evaluations systems were increasingly given to outside contractors, consulting firms and independent consultants in the belief that external specialists could do the work more efficiently and effectively than company itself.

Nowadays, there is a growing stream of organizations need to research into the outsourcing of innovation activities within the innovation, management, marketing and economics disciplines. These organizations need to understand how with the outsourcing practice becoming more commonplace in their industry. However, their behaviors bring these two questions: Whether outsource or internalize innovation activities and the performance implications of this decision can support for both transaction cost and resource based arguments is examined with both theory bases showing substantial attention? Whether outsourcing innovation activities can lead to faster product development and cost savings? On advantages hand, it is possible that outsourcing may lead to higher costs and slower new product development. Further the technological uncertainty may have conflicting impacts on the outsourcing decision that are not yet well understand. When outsourcing product development has reduced costs and has proved speed to market. On disadvantages hand, outsourcing has also reduce product development time delays and higher quality concerns. Why to cause performance implications of outsourced innovation activities in transaction in cost economics and the resource-based view point? When outsourcing product development has been to reduce costs and has improved speed to market, outsourcing product development is not unlike other make or buy decisions. So, make vs buy decision is similar to logistic and IT outsourcing. Internalization of product development will be preferred when transaction costs are excessive. Otherwise, the market i.e. outsourcing will be selected when transaction costs are low. Transaction costs can include adaption, safeguarding and measurement costs. Adaption costs represent efforts to adjust contract to change conditions and are a result of environmental uncertainty. When a firm may have to revise on agreement with a partner company, this facing substantial penalties, due to an unstable market environments, the firm is likely to perform this function internally. Safeguarding costs characterize the costs of an outsourcing provider acting opportunities after investments have been made in the inter-firm relationship and are the result of transaction specific investment. Measurement costs include all expenses with confirming that contracts have been fulfilled passably. The contracting firm may face substantial costs to estimate quality for contractual services. When the sum total of these transaction costs is substantial, internalization will be favored.

●

What is environmental uncertainty factor?

Environmental uncertainty refers to unanticipated changes in circumstances surrounding an exchange in market uncertain and technological uncertainty. Market uncertainty is the fluctuation and unpredictability of demand. With respect to innovation projects, market uncertainty may cause frequent changes to the development, complications and adding expense to external contracting. These changes may necessitate renegotiation or cancellation of innovation contracts, which will likely carry prohibitive penalties (a term) transaction costs. These transaction costs promote internalization under high levels of market uncertainty. Otherwise, technological uncertainty environments, selecting market governance allows firms the flexibility to end relationship should technical requirements shift. It seems that market and technological external change factor will influence to benefits to any organizations to choose outsourcing strategy. On the other side, outsourcing can bring this question: Whether the offshore outsourcing of information technology jobs choice is suitable to any IT organizations? Nowadays. The offshore outsourcing if IT jobs from the United States has been enabled by a powerful influence of global economic demographic and technological forces. In fact, many IT companies were drawn to offshoring outsourcing because of the need for programmers to fix the Y2K problem in the late 1990- year. It is shortages of US programmers. Other factors driving this phenomenon include the wage gap between the US and developing countries, e.g. China and India, advances in technology, labor availability, expanding foreign markets and foreign government incentives. The spread of the offshoring phenomenon from low skill manufacturing to high wage white collar service industry jobs reduces the country's IT jobs critics, it represents the mobility for many US workers who saw post-secondary education as the route to a higher standard of living. The offshoring outsourcing of manufacturing and service jobs from the US to lower cost foreign nations become a national issue in a very short time. The impact of offshore outsource on the information technology sector gives outsourcing potential loss of millions of jobs at all wage levels and the critical contribution is the IT sector to US productivity growth. However, decisions about the locations of manufacturing or service facilities reflect market forces key factors include the size of local markets, capital availability and costs, labor availability skill levels and cost, logistic issues, reliability and infrastructure and IT in particular relationships with research institutions. All these factors will influence the choice of offshore outsource IT jobs strategy top any organizations.

Whether outsourcing will bring
what kind of work skills.

Whether outsourcing will bring what kind of work skills. Many employers choose outsourcing to employ employees. This core of our work is identifying trends which will transform global society and the global marketplace. How it influences our nature of work form health care to technology, the work place and human identity. A decade ago, workers worried about jobs being outsourced overseas. Today companies, such as Odesk and Liveops can assemble teams " in the cloud" to dosales, customer support and many other tasks. It seems outsoucring can influence many high technological job of changes. Global connectivity, smart machines and new media are just some of the drivers reshaping how we thank about work, what constitutes work and the skills, we shall need to be productive contributors in the future. As computer technology in the cloud will be used popularly to society. A signal is typically a small or local innovation that has the potenial to grow in scale and geographic distribution. A signal can be a new product, a new practice, a new market strategy, a new policy or new technology, such as online cloud computing files storage service method. It is an innovative social science method to computer users. However, this new computer files storage method influences outsourcing service of needs increasing. It will have key drivers and skills areas that will be most relevant to the technological workforce of the future.

It is estimates that by 2025 year, the number of Americans over 60 age will increase by 70%. The challenge of an aging population will come. What it means to age, individuals will need to rearrange their approach to their career, family life and education to accommodate their life plan. Increasing, people will work long past 65 age in order to have adequate resources for retirement. Multiple careers will be commplace and lifelong learning to prepare for occupational change will see major growth. To take advantage of this well experienced organizations will have to rethink the traditional career paths in organizations, creating more diversity and flexibility. As the high technological cloud computing storage method is invented. Any organizations can save their files to the central cloud computer storage system website to save or find their files from website more easily. It will reduce their computer department expenditure and staff salary. So, outsourcing computer file storage service demands will be influenced to increase to any organizations as well as organizations will reorganize their computer department job nature to shape the kinds of social, economic and political organizations which inhabit. Outsourcing is a good solve method to assist organizations to pay cheap salary to employ many retired high age workers by contract or temporary or part time method to reduce their computer department's number of employees and the retired labors only need to pay cheap salary to learn how to use internet to help whose employers to save their files to their outsourcing computer storage service provider's central computer storage system every day efficiently. So, organizations do not need to employ many computer department staffs to avoid to pay much salaries to this computer department expenditure. They can choose outsourcing to pay cheap salaries to employ many retirement labors to assist them to do simple office storage job from internet channel efficiently and effectively. Hence, internet high technological innovation can influence office outsoucing of job duties increasing.

Whether domestic outsoucing in the America, what assesses trends and effects on job quality. Nowadays, US firms' use of contractors and independent contractors and its effect on job quality and inequality. Why firms choose contract out for certain functions and assess their predictions about likely impacts on job quality, stagnant wages, growing inquality and the deterioration of job quality are among the most important challenges facing the US economy today. Although any country's domestic outsourcing , firms' use of contractors, franchises and independent contractors any one of these factors is a potentially important influence to companies reduce compensation and shift economy risk to workers. However, the domestic outsoucing takes place on a much larger scale and effects many more workers than has been recognized ranging from low wage service workers, security guards, warehouse workers and hotel housekeepers to professionals and technical workers, such as programmers, health care technicians and accountants. These tends are part of structural change in the organization of production to influence quality of jobs and the nature of employment contract after outsourcing jobs are popular. The quality of jobs include wages, benefits, employee skills and training and mobility opportunities and job security as well as inequality across jobs. Domestic outsoucing concerns these issues: such as employment and labor law, the provision of health, pension and other workplace benefits. However, any companies choose outsourcing of employment reasons include, such as that it relates how management choices to pursue value added or cost focused strategies. Contracting out is difficult to define because a large part ot economic activity has always occurred through business-to-business transactions, as captured in macro-economic input-output models. Outsoucing job employment method can influence any one labor's individual quality of jobs. Usually, international companies choose the offshoring of work in global supply chains. Until recently, the domestic counterpart outsourcing employment method has grown supply chains to domestic or regional outsoucing employment.

What factors cause domestic outsourcing and whether firm decisions about what to retain in-house and what to outsource have changes over time. Some evidence suggests that firms have responded by focusing on their core competencies and outsourcing low value added tasks as well as higher value added specialized functions. Advanced technologies have facilitated this process by allowing firms to outsource entire functions ans more easily monitor contractors as well as employees who work, leading to new forms of networked production and rise of specialized outsouring employment firms. Domestic outsoucing influences the changes of job quality, benefits, hours, workload, job stability, schedule stability and occupational safety, health, incidence of wage theft and access to training and promotions. Predictions are less clear for job requiring professional or technicial or specialized skills or those that are outsourced to large and diversified outsourced contractors. Types of outsourced contracts include:

suppliers or vendors of products, such as manufacturing inputs or services, such as business services or staffs service or staffing firms, franchisees and independent contract, such as freelancers, independent contracts or non demand platform outsourced workers. It is significant restructuring of domestic manufacturing supply chains will greater reliance on suppliers and subcontractors. In addition, the potential growth of on demand outsourcing work as well as other forms of job fragmentation. It causes this question: How outsourced workers are multiple forms of income generating work to achieve economic security and how outsourcing workers can build career across jobs and over time.

Firm in every sector of the economy contract with other firms as part of their production process, as do governmental entities. The functions that are outsourced vary widely. For example: human resources ans research and development functions, building services, recycling, regulation and compliance, accounting, credit card collection, call centres, mortage and check processing, information technology and data processing, logistics and transportation, machine maintenance, cable installation, food services, food processing, parts manufacturing and assembly, laundry and housekeeping etc. outsourced jobs causes.

Whether what business impact of outsourcing will be caused? Nowadays, IT outsourcing was clearly a part of an effective management strategy that the companies felt IT outsourcing strategy can bring to achieve positive results. Information technology outsourcing providing servicers will be predicted to provide services that is expected to raise over the next five years minimum. The companies demand clients expected benefits of IT outsourcing and determined that cost reduction, increased operation, efficiency and improved IT effectiveness. What are the impacts of outsourcing to influence better long-term improvement in the business performance? It is impossible to being benefits of significant reduction and lower growth in sellings, general and administrative expense to IT outsourcing company demand clients. Also, pre-existing corporate cultures are focused on business improvement to IT outsourcing company demand clietns. In the past researches, some economists indicated that points can be used to reflect the actual numbers increase or decrease in percent. However, their prior researches shows that prior to outsourcing, the annual growth in selling, general and administration expenses of eompanies in the study was already 4.2 points lower than sector medium. Moreover, within one to two years after IT outsourcing these companies improved even most. Annual growth in selling and general administrative expenses for them was 9.9 points lower efford to assist any IT outsourcing will have selling and administrative expenses for long term. Also, almost two-third of the companies studied outperformed in increased growth in return on asset two to three years after IT outsourcing commenced. Prior to outsourcing, the annual ROA growth rate for companies in the study ws 7.5 points lower than the sector median. After outsourcing, however these companies experienced 8.6 points higher median a substantial change of 16.1 points. Also, nearly two to third of the companies studied grew earnings faster than their peers. Two to three years after IT outsourcing, companies experienced an annual rate of growth in earnings 11.8 points higher than the growth rate of the sector median. Thus, it seems IT outsourcing can assist the IT outsourcing demand clients to reduce expenditure and to raise income both as the same time. Then, it will cause these questions to IT outsourcing demand clients. Is outsourcing influencing in an economic downturn to finance sector in the short term? Is the finance sector's renewed change for outsourcing just a temporary cost-cutting measure? Will today's economic climate initiate long term financial and productivity gains? Whether what are benefits and disadvantages of outsourcing finance sector IT. I shall demonstrate why outsourcing open source software support and maintenance can be a good choice to start. Firstly when company plans to budget cuts expenditures, IT outsourcing is often the first choice. For example in 2003 year, Zurich Financial services' sprawling IT department consisted of more than 7,500 employees. After posting a record loss of 3.4 billion the year before, Zurich decided to cut down on in those staff and outsource nearly half of its IT work. Outsourcing has successfully cut costs by 45 percent and cut the number of in house IT staff by 60 percent. Here are some of the benefits that companies enjoy when they outsource information technology functions to competent, reliable vendors.

In fact, it can be too expensive to maintain, company's own information technology, especially during a recession. Fortunately, many IT functions can be easily and efficiently outsourced, positively impacting individual company's bottom line. Employee costs are much higher than just salary and benefits, keeping employees happy, productive and busy takes time, effort and money. Although, many IT staffs will be dismissed, it will increase the unemployment ratio in societies. But, moving an IT service out of house means financial organizations don't have to worry about technology refresh costs in the future. It also cuts down on human resources requirements, specialist IT service provides which can provide the newest technologies and deliver quality service more than company itself in house information provides are the most effective to develop and implement and upgrade their clients' software or the launch on a new platform, due to the expert's time is wasted on day-to-day duties for whose other IT outsourcing demand clients. However, instead of IT outsourcing service outsourced offshoring in that service sector, how economic impact to influence the outsourced offshoring country. For example, United States continues to run an international trade surplus in services. Many Americans are particularly concerned about the loss of skilled, well paid jobs in such fields as computer programming and accounting etc. positions. These jobs seemed relatively secure at a time when many manufacturing jobs were being cost to import competition. Similarly, telephone call centers, once viewed as an esonomic development opportunity in some areas, increasingly are moving low wage countries, such as India and the Philippines. Thus, offshoring raises many questions for policymakers and general public. For example, which service jobs will be affected most by import competition. What are the likely effects of service-sector offshoring on U.S.A. output, employment and our standard of living, such as America? Is offshoring really a problem that requires restrictive government actions or are other kinds of policies more appropriate to give Americans or other countries the highest possible living standard?

The term of offshoring refers to the relocation of jobs and production to a foreign country. The relocated jobs and production could be at a foreign office of the same multinational company or at a separate company located abroad. In constrast, the term outsourcing doesn't necessary imply that jobs and production are relocated to another country. The major outsourcing service jobs include human resource, accounting and information technology etc. in-house service jobs in large organizations. However, the loss of service jobs and factory production is caused by offshoring is diffuclt to measure. It is also difficult to determine the impact of offshoring on total services employment in the United States or other countries. International trade in services covers a wide range of industries and activites. For example, travel and transportation includes travel expenditures, passenger fares and frieght and port services, royalties and license fees cover transactions including patents, copyrights, trademarks and other intangible proprietary rights to use, produce or distribute products. Other private services include many of these industries, such as education, financial services insurance, telecommunications and other professional services etc. Some economists indicated that occupational employment statistics for the Unisted States provided additional evidence that past service sector offshoring had been small. About 14 million service jobs were at risk of offshoring in 2000 year, when about 96 million service jobs had a low risk of ofshoring. The decline in the at-risk service occupations from 2000 year to 2002 year was about 218,000 jobs or roughly 109,000 jobs annually, relatively small number that is consistent with the estimates of McCarthy or Zandi. In percentage terms, employment in the at risk occupations fell at a faster rate from 2000 year to 2002 year than in the low risk occupations. This faster decline is consistent with offshoring activity, although the decline is consistent with other explanations as well, such as faster of technological change in industries employing the risk occupations or greater cyclical sensitivity in these industries. Because offshoring was not the only cause of job loss in the risk occupations, the number of jobs moved offshore was undoubtedly less than 109,000 jobs annually. However, the estimates may understate the total impact because domestic companies with expanding worldwide employment may have located may of their newly created jobs abroad even when they didn't reduce their US employment. Some of those foreign jobs might provide services to US customers and potentially foreign jobs might provide service to US . Conversely, the estimates may overstate the total job loss from offshoring of the foreign outsourcing of some support jobs prevents the loss of other domestic jobs by keeping US firms competitive in world markets. For example, cost reductions from offshoring IT jobs might help a US financial services company win foreign contracts, preserving many professionals and support jobs in the US.

Lower production costs in foreign countries are a major cause of service sector offering. Although, the costs of land and other resources may be cheaper abroad, but the main difference betweeb the US and developing countries is labor costs. There is a large gap in computer programmer wages between the US and other countries. Any organizational capital includes both physical capital, such as machinery and computers and human capital , such as skills and knowledge. The cost savings is come from offshoring also might be reduced if the firm needed to pay higher transportation and telecommunication costs or management spends more time on service quality and data security. Still, the much lower levels of wages ans benefits in developing countries suggests that many services can be produced abroad at lower cost. The in-house professional relocation of labor-intensive service activities, such as legal transcription services to countries with lower labor costs is consistent with economists' basic theory of international trade, comparative advantage. So, in-house outsourced professional service will be a corporative advantage, if the country's legal profession is poor level to compare with the another country. e.g. the skill in-house the legal professional labors of the developing country, such as China is poor educational level to compare with the developed country, such as US. So, if China large organizations chose to outsource themselves in-house legal service jobs to outsource offshoring to US legal professional lawyers to do. It can bring comparative advantage to China large outsourced in-house legal service organizations, due to these China outsourced large organizations can reduce to employ to pay too much salaries to these many in-house Chinese domestic lawyers and the US outsourced legal consultants whose can give more professional legal recommendation to serve to the China large organizations.

In conclusion, although offshoring strategy can increase unemployment chance for this disadvantge. But, all of outsourcing benefits weighs are more than the offsourcing disadvantages. However, outsourcing strategy can have these benefits to the outsourced service demanders. Such as outsourcing is no longer just about cost saving, it is also a strategic tool that may power the twenty first century global economy. Moreover, outsourcing can increase productivity and competitiveness, e.g. for every 1000 jobs British Airways sends to India , the airline saves $23 million, companies can devote a portion of their outsourcing savings to helping employees make job transitions, also leader can no longer afford to view outsourcing as a business tactic, it is now essential to remain competitive. On the world stage, workers now compete globally, so individuals must continually learn more to vie successfully with their peers worldwide, the average company only spends about 20% of the value of its outsourcing contracts to manage its relationship with the outsource provider. So, in the positive view point, outsourcing strategy can bring a potential primary driver of the global economy development. Although, outsourcing can also cause the raising of domestic unemployment chance. But companies may soon be more outsourced than in sourced, signifying a fundamental reorganization that will affect employees, managers, customers and executives. Customers' choice will increase product costs will drop and workers' roles will change. Finally, the most important, the developing country will earn comparative advantage from the developed country's employers' offshoring jobs provision. Thus, the developing country's unemployment rate will be reduced, then the global economy will be kept more balance fairly.

Reference

Abrahamson, E., & Rosenkopf., (1993). Institutional and competitive bandwagons: Using mathematical
modeling and a tool to explore innovation diffusion.
Academy of management review, 18(3), 487-517.
Hill, C.W.L. & Jones, G.R. 1995. Strategic management, An integrated approach. Boston: Houghtom Mif In.

EIGHT

ROBOTS WHETHER CAN HELP ORGANIZATIONS TO AVOID RESOURCE WASTE

To judge whether robots can help any organizations to avoid resources waste behavior. We need to know whether robots can own recyle function. How do robots helpthe environment? Robots can help reduce waste that is implemented by effectively sorting materials that can be recycled and put to use again. They can even help sort waste materials quickly and move efficiently than humans reduce the input power amd cost unsociated with such processes. However, robots also may help business organizations with recycling, instead of natural environment . For example, tobots may help organization facility cut operate resource cost and allowed to take on a second load of recyclables to sort throgh.

How robotic technology help organizations reduce waste? Advanced software has made it easier to plan out routes that can efficiently guide waste collecting the waste and recycling materials that need to be collected. It also makes collection more fuel efficient and reduces energy usage to any offices, plants, warehouses, business organizations. It seems that robots can help organizations to bring recycling advantages. We should definitely keep on teaching robots to recycle our waste, e.g. clean robotics makes waste management smart with a robotic trash can that automatically separates used and not used materials in workplace environment.

How to use technology to help reduce waste? There is no financial incentive to reduce waste. One of a few manufacturers of AI (arificial intelligence) powered recycling robots. We can imagine a future where waste-collectig robots will move through air land, and water, cleaning our natural environment, workplace environment conveniently. For example, now robots are being put on duty to help solve the environment pollution, material waste, recycling challenges. AI assisted robotis technology that can work with humans in workplace organizational environment to have robots to do a better job at sorting garbage and reduce the building materials is wasted, sorting trash is a dirty and dangerous job, recycling robots may help human to do thin kind of sorting trash job, even further atomic bombs soon could be delivered over intercontinental distances aboard " pick a back" multi-stage rockets by robotis assistance. So, in our future, robotic can be applied on those avoiding resource waste job aspects, such as degradation and resource depletion , reduce , reuse, recycle and recover, have always been needed to avoid resource waste to future global business organizations. When, AI machine learning and robotics could help us , more efficiently organization, digital tools and new business models.

How green robots are helping with environmental sustainablity?

Robots can help reduce waste that is implemented by effciently sorting materials that can be recycled and put to use again. They can even help sort waste materials quickly and most efficiently than humans reducing the input power and cost associated with such processes.

How robots may help organizations to avoid resource waste?

Waste robotics autonomous recycling technology integrates advanced waste technology to avoid the costly deployment to any organizational users, e.g. the clean sea robot is an autonomous, electric floating aqua-droue that sweeps and collects plastic trash that has collected in coastal areas. It uses a has collected in coastal areas . It uses a combination of computer vision and remote sensing basd on 3D laser scanning technologies . So, clean sea robots can bring sea environmental protection advantages to global seas. Future global sea environment protection organization must need its clean sea tasks helping.

Instead of clean sea rubbish aspect, robots can also help organizations to do digital waste management tasks, digital technologies and their current use in waste management transparent, more economic and more resource-efficient processes, better souring of current important robotis digital waste manaement, technological trends, are robotics,the internet of things, cloud, digital rubbish robotic can help organizations to reduce digital rubbsh easily. then, any organizational digital system can do more efficient tasks daily. Hence, robotics can help e-commerce organizations to do digital resource waste management tasks in order to provide high efficient online purchase services to any countries online buyers in short time.

How robots are applied to reduce waste in hotel organizations?

Reducing waste in hotels in within reach with the help of digital technologies. How are robots used in hotels? Throughout the hotels, robots are deployed to provide information, front desk services, storeage services as well as check in and cleck out services , with technology including voice and facial recognition. An example, of artifical intelligence in the hospitality industry is the use of AI to deliver in-person customer service. The robot is able to provide tourist information to customers who interact with it. Most impressively, it is able to learn from human speech and adapt to individuals. waste management in hotels is important or it is getting increasingly difficult to dispose of waste. Therefore, hotel resource management robots can help hotels to decrease cost of waste disposal as the start with: Using refillable dispensers for soaps, shampoos and conditioners.

Could hotel service robots help the hospitality industry on resource management of robotized hotels, e.g. avoding food waste in hotel robotized hotels, example restaurants robotics technology can help chefs measure, manage and reduce food wase. Morevoer, a restuaurant robots do not get waste and can perform to help chels measure, manage and reduce food waste easily. From a human resource management point of view, in that sense, robotisation may help automation and hotels to improve it service and reduce restaurant food waste cost.

NINE

MANAGEMENT SCIENCE ROLE SOLVES RESOURCES SHORTAGES

● What does management resource science mean ?
Although, management science could include the study of all activities of groups that means a management function, it generally include discovering, developing, defining and evaluating the goals of the organization and alternative policies that will lead towards the goals. So, management science is the broad interdisiplianary study of problem solving and decision making in human organizations with strong links to management economics, business , engineering , management consulting fields. Management science helps business to achieve golas using of organizational resources to produce goods and service. It

is a contemporary approach to management that is an extension of scientific management that measures the worker to task mix and ratio to raise efficiency.

Thus, the nature of management science is a science because it contains a systematic body of knowledge in the form of general principles. Management principles are important in nature, but they can not be expected to give same results in every suitation. Therefore, management is a social science. If any organizations feel resources are shortages, they need to find that the main factors to influence their resources are often shortage. Management science may be one kind the best management research choice, because it uses various scientific research-based principles, strategies and analytical methods including mathematical modeling, statistics and numerical methods to improve an organization's ability to enact rational and accurate management decisions by arriving at optional or near oprimal solutions to complex decision.

● Why does management science help organizations to avoid/solve resource shortage?

Because management is a core function of every business and a number of theories try to explain how any why resource will be use rapidly and resource shortage causes to any organization. The core function of the management science approach is to compare possible outcomes. In addition, managers in various functions have aware of the potential contribution of analytical modes . So, the managerical science function involves arranging equipment perform functions, such as procurement, production etc. activities.

For drug manufacturing organization or hospital, clinic, medical service organizations exmaple, any kinds of drug must be important resource to provide patients to eat. If they have not enough drugs to be provided to the hospital, clinic, medical service organizational patients to eat. Then, their sicknesses may become serious suddenly. So, managing enough drugs stick is very important. However, management science may help any one these medical organization to implement rationality in strategic decisions: Choice which kinds of drugs purchase number, in order to keep enough drugs supply in drug store room. Understanding in a drug resource pool choice, due to cash available is limited to any one medical organizations.

Management science aims to avoid drug shortage to any one medical organizations. Such as this drug organization case, management science may help them to identify the processes, which kinds of drugs are needed to buy immediately, notice the areas of weaknesses, and realize the future possibilities and needs of the medical organization's patient customers needs. The approach makes the drug utilization of resources easier, since the framework can notice the availability of drug resources and the proper eat of them to be provided to any sickness kinds of patients to eat immediately when the medical organization can have enough drug stocks supply.

How to apply management science to help hospital better prepare for a drug shortage management method may include: Having a plan, the director of pharmacy should consider developing a plan for managing drug shortages, implement structured communications. Ask the right questions,instead of , hospital management also needs to know what is causing drug shortages. IN fact, drug shortages are caused by many factors, including: regulatory issues, and business decisions as well as many other disturbances within the supply chain.

Hence, in management science view point, hospital can attempt to apply mobile App technolgies tool to solve drug shortage problem, because mobile App technologies tool can be one kind of immediate communication tool, it can identify when the kind of drug will shortage and their impact on hospitals, e.g. how many the kind of sickness patient number and automates the entire life cycle of managing any kinds of drug shortage. Mobile App, communication technologic tool can provide clinical information that allows teams to understand and mitigate the ramifications for shorted medications. Any possible drug shortage solution in hoepital, it may be a management strategy that includes clear policies and producers for information. It defines a drug shortage is as a supply issue that affects how the drug store room's daily drug supplies.

Thus, management science may help any medical organizations to solve drug shortage crisis, it may help any organizations to attempt to reduce health care cost, one common solution for mitigating shortages is to keep more drug inventory, but drug inventory number can not be excess, in order to avoid drug out of patients (old drug) to let patients to eat in difficult. Hence, any medical organizations need to implement good pharmaceutical supply chain management strategy in order to solve drug resolve shortage challenge causes.

● How to apply management science technological tool to solve resource shortage to organization challenge?

Management science technological tool predict method may also be applied to water scarcity management aspect for government water supply organization, it may provide the scientific basis to apply optimum water resource management practices in the affected areas, methodological procedure for drought and water scarcity management or applying the economic scarcity potential method to rare earth elements highlights. It can capture resource is a useful approach as is it has an technological tool to avoid scarcity of resources to farm from atmospheric physic to robotic farm water resource shortage technological tool. A key component of this farm management approach is the use of information gathering concerns weather change. It aims to help farmers can predict when ther are enough rain supply to the farm land, they ought grow rice or fruit seed or vegetabe seed to farms. hence, it seems that management science method may be applied to help any organizations to solve natural resource or manufacture resource supply shortage challenge to any organizations.

ON conclusion, management science may be applied to resource shortage aspect, because management science is resource management technique. The two techniques are as follows: resource technique is a technique in which start and finish dates are adjusted based on resource constraints with the goal of balancing demand for resources against available supply. Any organizations may encounter resource shortage challenge. Resource scarcity is essentially about current demand for a resource exceeding available supply. Resource scarcity occurs when demand for a natural resource is greater than the available supply , leading to a decline in the stock of available resource . However, any organizational resource shortage may due to failure management, difficult management technique causes. The common types of resource management may include human resource management natural resource management, project resource management, financial management, infrastructure management , facility management enterprise asset management public asset management at organizational resource management aspects. Hence any organizations must need efficient and effective resource management strategy in order to avoid resource shortage causes.

In organizational studies, resource management is the efficient and one resource management technique choice is resource shortage solution leveling, to keep the enough stock of resources on hand, reducing both excess inventories and shortages. Any kind of resource management technique aims to ensure access to resoures and avoid supply shortages efficiency in their use, facilitate their proper and of life management, hence, effective resource management strategy may help the organization to avoid resource shortge challenge causes easily.

● Reasons to organizations need management resource strategies ?

Why ought organization implement resource managment strategies ? better utilization means a happier and healthier team helping to reduce being overburdened and stressed. Resources are used to their maximum potential, keeping projects on time and on budget. It helps project managers keep to reduce oversights. The reasons that organizations ought to prepare effective managment science to implement the most reasonable and the most efficient and the most effective resource management strategy, because effectively managing resources can help companies more consistently deliver projects and services on time.

This is because better resource management helps to improve insights into resource availability as well as improves timelines projections. Why it is importsant to have enough resources supply and resource management strategies implementation? Resources are important for the growth to one organization, even development for any country, for example, generate energy , one need fossil fuels, and for industrial with the development, we require mineral rsources . On macro-social development aspect, natural resources are getting scarce with the increasing populatin, so it is essential to conserve them.

Why do we need resource management to organizations ? Resource management is the process of pre-planning, scheduling, and allocating the kind of resources to maximize efficiency. A resource is anything that is needed to eecute a task or project, this can be the skill set of employees or the adoption of software. Due to large organizations might be dealing with multiple projects. Effective allocation of resources help project maangers to avoid to use resources inefficiently, e.g. human resources, financial resource, physical resource and information resources. Hence, effective resource management science strategy can benefit the organization team and overall organization.

● How applying right science resource management principle to organizations

Scientific management is an attitude and a philosophy to be accepted and applied of the method of scientific investigation for the solution of the problems of industrial management . They may include experimentati, collection of data, analysis of data and formaulation of certain principles on the basic of such analysis. It aims to seek the most efficiency for plant operations. The main objective is improving economic efficiency, especially labour productivity.

However, scientific management can be summarized in

four main principles to determine and standardize the one best way of doing a job . A clear division of tasks and responsibilities. High pay for high performing employee, for Toyalor's scientifi managmement principle example, he proposed that by optimizing and simplifying jobs, productivity would increase.

Nowadays, most organizations in the industry make use of scientific management, e.g. hospitals, car and computer , restaurants, among others. The advantages may include : reduction in the cost of production, better quality products, benefits of division of labour , avoidance of disputes between labour and management increased wage, gains to owners/investors.

The main aim of scientific management is to develop all men to their greatest efficiency . The specific objectives aim to enhance production and productivity, decrease cost of production and maximize prosperity both for employer and employees having common interests (not opposite to each other).

● How Amazon e-commerce applies resource management principle to bring avoiding resource waste benefit?

For Amazon e-commerce example, it does not apply scientific management principle, due to it is not one product manaufacturing industry, it is online sale service and foreign delivery service organization. It ignores one of the key of scientific management, its creators genuinely believed that you had to pay higher wages to anyone asked to puch themselves to their physical limits. Under scientific management wages are paid to the workers as per the piece-wage system. Minimum wage is not assured, so every work needs to pay incentive wafe when he can manufacture more piece product, but Amazon believes that pay higher wages to any one can bring incentive productivity , such as it only provide online sale and foreign deli ery service to any one online buyer client, e.g. it can pay higher wage to the warehouse workers, because they need to cooperate with robotics to work hard and the human warehouse workers need to learn how to dominate any one warehouse logistic robotics to know hoe to delive and put goods to the right shelves in order to avoid to put wrong goods to the not right shelves position in warehouse.

So, in Amazon scientific management skill to workers view, its warehouse workers are smart workers, they need to know how to dominate any one warehouse robotics to do the right goods delivery to put on right shelves tasks daily. Their wages ought need to pay higher in order to avoid theig goods wrong delivery to wrong sheleves in careless. SO, Amazon feels that it needs to pay higher salary to the warehouse workers because they need have more smart and robotic control skills. When they and robotic to works together in Amazon warehouses.

So, such as Amazon warehouse workers case, Amazon ecommerce organization can apply scientific management principle to reduce resource waste. I shall explain as below: Amazon 's warehouses have save diffeent kinds of products to prepare to deliver to different countries buyers, after Amazon had confirmed that it has receive visa card payment from online channel by each online buyer successfully. So, it must have smart warehous workers, they know how to control and dominate any one warehouse robotics to cooperate to send every right shelf position message to every one warehouse robotis to know, when the warehouse robotic receives the right product delivery to the right shelf message from the warehouse warehouse, it will delvier the product to the shelf position carefully. So, avoiding none of any wrong goods putting on the wrong shelves positions occurs easily. When, every one, there has none any wrong goods are putted on wrong sheleves positions occurrence, the spending investigation time to any wrong goods putting on wrong shelves position, it does not need to any one warehouse manager to do every day, So, Amazon does not need to waste time to do any goods putting on wrong warehouse workers number, when it applies many warehouse robotics to assist them to work in order to raise goods delivery efficiency in warehouse, e.g. Amazon warehouse can apply three logistic robotics and one human warehouse worker number to do one goods shelf delivery task. Before, it needs to employ ten human warehouse, logistic workers to reponsible to do one goods shelf delivery task. I assume that the goods shelf can put total 300 pieces of different kinds of products per day. So, Amazon can reduce none warehouse logistic workers number when it increases three logistic robotics to help them to do these 300 goods delivery task per day. Hence, its wage expenditure must decrease. Moreover, logistic robotics do not feel tried , bored, overtime work, these three robotics only follow any one of warehouse worker's message to let them to know whether which kind of product is needed to put on which number of the shelf positiion. Then, these three logistic workers can remember where the product is putted on the shelf position and help any one logisitic worker to get the right product to already deliver to the foreign buyer's home from Amazon's warehouses easily, they must raise efficiency more than only workers , they work in Amazon warehouses.

Hence, Amazon believes higher wage can enourage smart logistic workers can have good performance to dominate how every logistic robot , e.g. avoiding to send wrong message to let any one logistic robotic to put wrong product to the wrong shelf number position. SO, Amazon can apply warehouse scientific management method to avoid warehouse worker individual wrong message delviery to any one logistic robotic occurrence, when they can receive higher wage, and the three logistic robotics and one warehouse worker cooperation relationship is the most suitable workers cooperation number.

Amazon 's warehouse does not need more nine workers to often move in the crowd warehouse space environment to avoid worker accident and wrong goods putting on wrong shelves number position occurrences both. Hence, Amazon can apply scientific management method on warehouse avoiding resource waste aspect, when it decides to apply logistic robotics and workers cooperation in order to avoid wasting time to investigate whether which kinds of goods are put on where the wrong shelves number positions per day tasks occurrence in possible and it can bring delay to deliver goods to the online buyer's home. it is one good example of scientific management avoiding time waste method to Amazon warehouse organization.

TEN

Can Robotic Help Warehouses To Avoid Resource Waste On Behavioral Economic View

● Behavioral economy view whether robotic can help warehouse to avoid time and human resource
waste

IN fact,robts are being used in different types manufacturing to create more efficiency with fewer resource. Robots also reduce errors, to leass waste is produced. Less waste is produced and the robots are able to final and separate the small parts more efficiently than human hands can. For example, on environment recycled aspect, robots can help reduce waste that is incinerated by efficiently sorting materials that can be recycled quickly and more efficiently than humans reducing the input poser and cost control with such processes. So, robots can bring positive affect the environment, because robots use less energy and produce less waste.

As a whole, there are multiple benefits to using robots to fight climate change,e.g. robots can prevent pollution and emissions through careful monitoring optimize the manaufacturing processes to reduce energy consumption. Moreover, robots can help with recycling, the use of robots allows facility operators some new flexibility. Most technologies used in recycling allow to sort materials. The sensing robots (sensoes) allow robots to receive information about a certain measurement of the environment , or internal components. This is essential to robots to perform their tasks, and act upon any changes in the environment to calculate the appropriate response.

● How Amazon warehouse applies logistic robots to help

it to waste resource waste

Hence, although robots can take our jobs, because they can help organizations to avoid resource waste, and it can bring negative effect to influence we lose jobs. ON behavorioral economic view, robots can help employers to reduce employees number, but it won't influence organizational overall performance to be worse or inefficiency, such as Amazon warehouse applies logistic robots to assist workers to deliver the right kind of goods to put on every correct shelf number position rapidly every day. Hence, one logistic robot can replace at least 10 store workers to do goods delivery tasks every day, e.g. one store worker needs to spend one minute to find the right kind of good to deliver to prepare to arrange to deliver it to fly to overseas client. Logistic robots only need 10 seconds to find the right kind of goods from the near 200 number shelves in Amazon warehouse as well as they are putting 300 different kinds of goods on these 200 shelves in Amazon warehouse every day.

Because each logistic robot has very good memory. Each logistic robot must remember any kinds of goods , their putting number position on which shelf, e.g. when the worker needs to find the model laptop product from 300 different kinds of products,in Amazon warehouse. They are putting on 200 number shelves number following positions. IN general, human worker will need to spend about one minute to find the model of laptop product from these 200 number shelves in warehouse. For example, when one worker needs to find the brand Apple of one laptop product model: PHZ0123, when the warehouse has total 300 diferent kinds of products are putting on total 200 numbers of different shelves positions. Any one Amazon store worker must need to type this Apple brand laptop" Apple" name and its model number" PHZ0123 on the store computer as well as to search its putting on shelf number position from computer. Then, the Amazon store computer will find this laptop product to find its present putting on the correct shelf number position , e.g. 50 number of the shelf positon, or none stock record of all this model PHZ20123 laptop is sold out. So, Amazon store computer must need time to help this store worker to search this laptop product's putting on shelf number position as well as the worker needs time to walk to the right shelf number position to find this laptop product.

However, logistic robotic does not need to spend time to type this laptop product brand name and model number in order to search where it is putted on the shelf number position. The Amazon store worker only needs to speak this laptop product brand name, e.g. Apple and the kind of product, e.g.laptop and model number, e.g. PHZ0123 and its piece number, e.g. one piece number. Then, the Amazon logistic robot can follow the store worker's sound to find its past this kind of product's shelf number position memory to move to this shelf correct number position and finds it to deliver to the worker immediately. So, if the worker speaks 10 kinds f different products one time, then the logistic robotic can help this worker to find these 10 of different kinds products from their correct shelves numbers rapidly. Hence, it seems that logistic robots can help Amazon store workers to reduce each product search time as well as logistic robots can help workers to do goods delviery tasks. So, in logistic robotic behevioral economic vire, logistic robotics can replace many workers to do product position research and delivery tasks, store workers only need to speak the kind of product name, model, brand name and delivery piece number to let the logistic robotic to know. Then, the logistic robotic can follow the store worke's sending message to find the product's past memmory in order to tell the store worker, whether the product has how many stocks on shelf, or none of stock on shelf and where is putted on . Hence, any one store worker does not need to spend much time to search where any kinds of products shelves number position are. They only need logistic robotics to help them to do any kinds of products deliver to , or 20 or more different kinds between products location and the store worker's location. It means that the store worker only needs to stay on the same location to wait the logistic robotic brings his products comes back after he speaks to let the logistic rotic to know whether which kinds of products and piece number he needs . Then, he checks the logistic robotic's all products where they are correct or not. He may put all of these different kinds of gatherng products to the lorry to prepare to send to airport to fly to another country to deliver to the overseas client's home immediately when he confirms that all goods are his correct.

Hence, such as Amazon warehouse case, logistic robotics can help it to reduce many products searching time tasks and avoiding delivering wrong product to any overseas client's home rick occurence. Also, logistic robotics can reduce store workers number, because logistic robotics can replace 10 to 20 human store workers number absolutely. Otherwise, human store workers may have errors in their product search process, e.g. finding the wrong product from shelf or putting the product to the wrong shelf number position, but logistic robotics can reduce to 0 error to put wrong product on the shelf number position or spends long time to search the kind of product from the shelf number position. So, in logistic robotic behavioral economic view, robotics can help businesses to avoid products putting on wrong shelves number position error risk, reduce store workers number, reduce product shelf number position search economic time.

ELEVEN

ORGANIZATIONAL INTANGIBLE RESOURCE MANAGEMENT STRATEGY

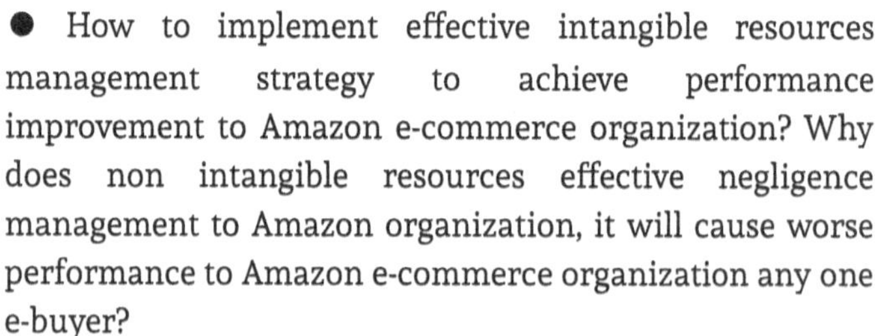

● How to implement effective intangible resources management strategy to achieve performance improvement to Amazon e-commerce organization? Why does non intangible resources effective negligence management to Amazon organization, it will cause worse performance to Amazon e-commerce organization any one e-buyer?

One efficient organization must need have efficient and effective resources management strategy in order to provide enough resources for its organization overall different departments cooperation effectively and efficiently. How to implement effective resources management strategy to achieve performance improvement? Why does ersources shortage to organization, it will cause worse performance? I shall explain the reasons as below:

For Amazon e-commerce organization example, it is one global the most large goods transport delivery service moddleman role between global online customers and their product salespeople. Amazon owns its webstores, so global any one country buyer clicks to its different countries webstores , then he/she can choose any kinds of products to buy from Amazon any one country webstore. However, the product is owned the another seller. So, any products are not owned by from Amazon any one country webstores. However, the product is owned by the another seller. SO, any products are not owned by Amazon. It only provides webstores to let global any one e-buyer to buy the product after he/she has paid visa payment. So, Amazon's role is one middleman. It needs to provide goods transport service to help the product's seller to deliver the product to whose e-buyer individual hoime in the most short time, e.g. when one China e-buyer clicks to Amazon China webstore , after he chooses any brands of computers product from Amazon China webstore, he makes purchase of the brand of comouter decision. Then, he needs to pay visa to Amazon 's China webstore . When Amazon confirms that ie can accept payment by the China e-buyer's visa. Then, Amazon will deliver the product to the China e-buyer's home within one week or longer time, the delivery days time depends on how much delivery fee, the China's e-buyer , he can pay. So, Amazon only can receive commision infomr from the computer brand product seller. Because Amazon can build famous loyalty of rapid goods delivery service provider barnad and its different countries websites can provide above one million different kinds of brand products to let global different conuntries eObuyers to choose in order to make the most fair and the most reasonable purchase price decision from its different Amazon different countries webstores per day. So, Amazon can help its different countries sellers to apply Amazon itself unique different countries' websotes design to attract global many different countries e-buyers to click to Amazon's webstores to find any kinds of products to choose to buy conveniently.

So, such as Amazon e-commerce organization case, if it hopes to attract global different countries e-buyers prefer to click to Amazon itself any one webstore more than other firms themselves webstores . Then, it must need have enough resources (tangible and intangible) both in order to provide raoid goods delviery service and many different kinds of goods choice provision service and reasonable price consumption channel to let any one countrye-buyer feels confidence and safe payment transaction and enough product advertisement, photo, price, function information in order to make final purchase decision from Amazon itself different country webstores more easily.

Hence, the tangible and intangible resources are needed to supuply to Amazon e-commerce organization. They may include: Product photos, price information, product advertisement which are shown to Amazon's different countries webstores , enough online customer service enquiry employees number, enough computers number, enough computers number, different countries offices and warehouses number, computers, internnet technology etc. tangible resource as well as customer service enquiries feedbacks, global rapid goods delivery transport service to any one country e-buyer's home, safe e-payment channel, providing to buy global any one country sellers their products in the most reasonable and the most fair purchase transaction. All ot these issues are any one e-buyer individual purchase feeling to Amazon. SO, they are intangibel (non-tangible) resources to Amazon. It means that if Amazon can let global any one e-buyer feels it's e-purchase service provision can let they feel more satisfactory , then they will choose to buy Amazon webstores any kinds of products more than other sellers their webstores products, because Amazon webstores can provide the kind of product of different brands choice, it aims to compare whether which brand's price is unreasonable too high or which brand's product's quality is worse, or design is not very atrraction. So, Amazon's intangibale resource, such as rapid goods delivery service, online or phone customer enquiry service, webstores' products information whether e-buyers can feel satisfactory, e.g. reasonable price, clear product photo many different kinds of brands product choice. All of these intangible resources to Amazon, they may also influence Amazon's future e-buyer number absolutely.

● How can Amazon raise intangible resource number to be effective?

SO, I explain that Amazon hadboth kinds of resources. They may include tangible and intangible resources. Internet speed, whether it is intangible resources. Internet speed, whether it is rapid or slow to satisfy global e-buyers online purchase speed and non online traffic jam accidents feeling. Amazon webstores any brands of products, photos, price information images whether they are clear to let any one global ebuyer to feel when they click to Amazon any one webstores. All of these internet technology resources to Amazon any one webstore will influence Amazon e-commerce organization's e-buyers number will increase or decrease . For example, if Amazon's China webstore can not let Chinese e-buyers to feel that it can not provide different kinds of brand products photos' clear image to let any one Chinese e-buyer to see the product photo clearly. When one Chinese e-buyer clicks to Amazon Chinese webstore to find any brands of laptop products to prepare to choose one to buy. But when he clicks to Amazon China webstore, he can not feel any one brand of laptop's photo is clear to let he feels. Then, theser unclear laptop photos may influence the Chinese e-buyer forgets his laptop purchase decision from Amazon 's China webstore easily. He may clcik to the another brand of laptop seller webstore to buy the brand of laptop from the laptop seller itself webstore. SO, Amazon's webstore design may be the important intangible resource to influence global any one e-buyer's visiting Amazon's any one webstore times or reducing to do to choose to visit Amazon's webstore behavior , due to they do not click to Amazon any one webstore websites again.

I recommend that Amazon ought consider how to design its any countries webstores in order to attract global e-buyers visiting Amazon itself webstores times number increase. So, global e-buyers' visiting Amazon different countries webstores times which will be Amazon's most important intangible resources to cause its future global e-buyers number. This kind of intangible resources may help Amazon e-commerce goods delivery service organization to raise its competitive effort,, because when one country's ebuyer feels Amazon can provide the most attraction and fair purchase channel from its different countries webstores. Then, the country's e-buyer will talk to his friends, families to prefer to choose Amazon if they have online purchase desire. Because Amazon's any one e-buyer , he .she will persduade his/her friends, families to choose Amazon's e-purchase channel., if he feels it can provide excellent e-purchase method to satisfy his online purchase need. Consequently, Amazon's e-buyers number may be influenced to increase.

ON conclusion, such as Amazon case, how to decide its whether which is the most important tangible and/or intangible resources in order to raise competition effort. It depends on whether how the seller sells its product, in order to concentrate on spending to increase the kind of resources number, such as Amazon e-commerce goods sale and delivery service organization case, internet webstores design intangible image dissatisfactory or satisfactory feeling which may be the most influential global e-buyers number increases or decreases. Moreover, Amazon's internet webstores design intangible satisfactory or dissatisfactory feeling resource may also influence e-buyer before or after e-purchase service requiry feedback feeling, safe visa card payment feeling, fair and reasonable brands of products price information and different brands of product photos image seeing satisfactory or dissatisfactory feeling , they are intangible resource asset to Amazon when global any one ebuyer must need to click to its any one webstore to find its any kinds of product to make purchase decision. So, any organizations must need to spend limit money to support its the most influential intangible resource , instead of tangible resources in order to increase clients number.

On conclusion, we can increase organizational resources on these several aspects: Organizational resources are all assets that are available to a firm for use during the production process or service process, such as Amazon ecommerce organization case. The four basic types of organization resources are human, monetary, raw materials may be tangible, but internet technology may be another intangible resource to today any organizations. Improving organizational resources aim to improve efficiency, it means as the ability to accomplish something with the least amout of wasted time, money and effort or performance as well as effectiveness, such as improving internet speed, and none online traffic jam accidents occurrence easily. It means as trhe degree to which something is successful in producing a desired result success. However, we can improve resources by these way, they may include : Review who manages resources within the organization, build an-up-to date knowledge raise and company wide resource pool, manage the resource pool in line with the market, focus on education and talent employees growth, keep the customers in mind, work on quality services or products, learn to use technology , such as Amazon needs to learn how to raise high speed internet service for its webstores, and avoid online traffic jam frequent occurrent to its any one country webstore.

To sum up effective resource management strategy can help any organizations to increase resource number. Resource management is acquiring , allocating and managing the reosurces, such as individuals, and their skills, finances, technology , material , machinery, and natural resources required for a project. Hence effective effective resource management strategy ensures that internal and external resources are used effectively on time and budget, resources may be obtained internally from the host organization or procured from external resources. SO, effective resource management can help organizations to save resources being wastes and finances being spend on the wrong things, a significant cost saving factor. Hence, such as Amazon e-commerce organization, it needs to know how to learn how to apply internet technology to improve its different countries webstores design, shorten goods transport delivery time, gathering more different brands of product prices, data and phoducts photos improving safe visa card transaction secret to increase e-buyer individual e-purchase confidence. When Amazon can concentrate on effective allocate limited resource to achiev ethese objectives. Then, its global e-buyer number may increase significantly.

TWELVE

US Space Science Research Organization (NASA) Resource Management Strategy

Why does intangible resource may influence NASA organization successurce management strategy

In global space science research industry, it is only one space science research organization in US , this organization establishmenet aims to investigate whether our earth outside has natural resource supplies, e.g. water , air, for example research moon, had been past US apce science research mission, following this US space science research will have unlimited number of any new space science research missions. However, if futuse use sapce science research organization hopes to continue to carry out on researching any new space planets missions in success, e.g. continue researching whether our earth outside has natural resource, e.g. fresh water, air existence in any large, or amll size planets, even their distrances are long away to our earth. Hence, their space science research organization whether it has enough tangible and intangible resources supplying factor as well as how it impkements its resoruce management strategy in order to use resource achieve to carry on researching any new space science research missions efficiently and effectively .

These both issues will be further space scienece research organizaions' main successful factor. So, I shall attempt to explain hw US space science research ourganizaion oughr achieve its resource management strategy in rder to achieve any difficult space science researching missions to be more simple.

NASA was for national aeronautics and space administration NASA to a US government agency that is responsive for science and technology related to air and space. The space age started in 1957 with the launch NASA missions, they are organized work to planetary science, hellophysics, and astrophysics. In NASA organizational structure , the administrators and deputy administrators of NASA are the highest ranked oficials of NASA , the space agency of the US government.

The administrator serves as the senior space science advise of the president of the US . SO, this NASA administrators has authorities to manage their organization;s any kinds of intengible and tangible resources how to be used. However, NASA's organizational structure is based on two primmary levels of managment responsibility. The first is agency management which primarily resides at headquarters. The second is stategic entreprise management which includes managing centers ans programs. so these two departments must have much authorities to manage how any organizational resources to be use for NASA's any space science research missions. However, if they can manage resources efficiently, they can help NASA organiztations to void resources wastes to any further space science research missions . SO, resource management strategy is very important to influence NASA organizations's success or failure, because if it has enough resources to achieve any planned space science research missions, then they can not achieve effectively. SO, resource management strategy is very important to NASA organization.

Global environment protection resource management strategy

On global environment protection resource management strategy aspect, NASA global conserves and protects natural resource through world class habitat and species management programs to our earth natural environment. It reduces the threatened and endangered species by poor natural environment were of ecological , recreational, aesthetic, education and scientific value to the nation's public . The enhancement of the environment, and is a procedural statute for application by the federal agencies. Hence, NASA organization believes that it needs to learn how to protect our earth natural resource to avoid waste and it brings to influence our earth ecological environment to become more worse. Then, we and our animals can not live comfortable .So, if this most simple protection to our earth's natural environment, NASA can do, then it must have effort to implement the most effective resource management stategy to avoid resource waste or use the least resource to carry on any space science research mission effectively.It seems that how to learn reduce our earth's natural environment resources, NASA can know how to spend or use the least resources to implement any further space science researth missions effectively.

Hence, I feel that NASA is one learning organization, have to help our earth to reduce natural organization waste, even how to manage resources to implement and new space science research mission to be used effectively. It is difficult to general business organizations, they only consider how to earn more profit aim. Otherwise, NASA does not provide effective checks and balances, does not have an independent safety program, and has not demostrated the characteristics of a learning organization. So, NASA is responsible for learning to educate human's fishing or farming businesses can avoid to influence our environment natural resource waste, even it is implemening resource management strategy to save our earth to avoid natural resource waste, e.g. oil, gas protection resource won't have enough supply issus occurrence.

Why does NASA need to be a learning organization?

In fact, learning has always been at the core of NASA 's project management successes and failures. Throughout, its history, the agency and its external stakeholders have conducted periodic studies of the importance of learning from proven best practices in project management. SO, learning effort , it must be NASA organization's intangible resource, it needs have good knowledge management strategy to prepare to learn any new methods to help it to solve any further new space schience resarch mission.

It means that knowledge managagement strategy will ne NASA's effective resource management method. It is only way to help NASA to solve any resource management challenges , when it encounters any difficulties to any space science research missions. Has knowledge management (KM) resource strategy to NASA organization relationship to resource mangement? The KM resources collection is comprised of critical knowledge links and artifacts, instituational knowledge assets, lessos learned from missions and projects, than drive mission success can knowledge management impact to NASA organization's own resource manafement strategy before it implements any space science research missions?

In fact, the benefits of using knowledge managment which may help any organizations, they include improved organization resource manageement effort, better and faster decision making, quicker problem solving , increased rate of innovation, supported employee growth and development , sharing of specialist expertise, better communication, improved business processes. A knowledge management plan is an organized, systematic and focused approach to identifying and implementing the knowledge goals and objectives of a project. So, such as NASA must have many different prepared science research project to be prepared to implement. If it can have good knowledge management plan, used challenges to any one project more easily.

Hence, NASA must need have a good knowledge managment plan, it is organized, systematic and focused approach to identify and implementing the knowledge goals and objectives of any a space science resource project, it is a document for a specific space science research project, department or function, which details. So, NASA needs have effective systems of processes, technologies and roles will be used to manage knowledge withing every space science research mission project.

This, effective knowledge management strategy is the main knowledge management strategy is the main factor to influence NASA organization's further every space science research missions their successes or gailure. It seems that NASA's intangible resource "knowledge management" , it may be the main intangible asset to influence it's any space science research missions whether they can use the least human, money, equipment technology resource to achieve successfully. Even, knowledge management may help NASA organization increase successful rate to achieve any further of different kinds of difficult space science research missions , because when NASA organization can implement an effective knowledge management strategy to learn or improve or revise whether every tim failure to its space science research mission, what are tha main factors to cause their missions failure, e.g. not advanced space technology or space equipment, supplying factor, difficult or not accurate prediction to worse natural space environment, changing factor, not enough skilful training ro any learning time arrangement to one spaceman individual skillful factor, because any one time space science research mission failure, it may due to different not controlled such as space worse changing envioronment or controlled factor, such as not enough learning time to provide to skillful , however, to investigate whether what the main factor

THIRTEEN

EDUCATIONAL ORGANIZATION RESOURCE MANAGEMENT STRATEGY

● Reasons internet is important intangible resource to e-educational organization

Does global resource shortage influence educational organizational resource shortage? For example,global gas resource natural resource shortage, it may influence global gas sale organizations gas product supply number reduced, due to they won't have enough oil raw material to supply to manufacture gas product. So, it seems that they have cause and effect of gas supply and gas product increasing or decreasing price relationship between global oil raw material supply number and gas organizational any kinds of gas products sale number. However, I shall concentrate on discussing whether educational organizational teaching service provision, they will need to depend some resources existence or not, if it is true that global some educational organization will need to depend on some kind of resources, in order to provide their educational service performance more successful. Whether what kinds of resources factor may influence their educational service in success. I shall attempt to indicate examples to explain as below:

Nowadays, global educational service is very competitive. Some countries educational organizations began to apply internet technology to implemenbt distance learning educational service to provide online learning channel to any one overseas student to choose his/her distance learning course to learn. I suppose that internet technology is further learning new trend, it will assist different countries students. They do not need to fly to foreign any one country to learn moew conveniently. SO, they do not need to spend much expenditure to learn from oversea any one university. The expenditure may include air ticket go and return expenditure, foreign living cost, transport cost, food cost, rent cost. Although these distance learning students must still need to pay school fee to the distance learning country, but in fact, when the student chooses to learn from internet channel.

This internet learning channel must help the distance learning students to save much extra not essential living expense. Hence, when the university decides to apply internet technology to provide distance learning courses to let overseas student to learn. The internet technology must be the university's technology resources to keep its any distance learning degree courses, such as undergraduate, master and doctor degrees continue to implement to let any one country student may enjoy to study this overseas university's any high and low degree level courses from internet channel conveniently.

Hence, internet this kind of technology courses may influence whether future any one country's university can continue to implement it's distance learning degrees to let any one country's student to learn. It explains that why the university must need have 24 hours internet service to let global different countries students can follow different daily e-classroom time tables to carry on online learning as well as lecturers can also follow different daily e-classroom time tables to teach their students from online classrooms channel conveniently, hence, the providing distance learning university must need have efficient high speed internet technology facilities to provide e-learn resources to carry on any one classroom teaching service to let any one country's student to feel satisfactory to learn from its e-classrooms. If the university's internet facilities are poor, easy internet linking or rapid internet speed to let many different countries distance learning students to feel its e-classrooms have better performance to compare other distance learning universities competitors. Then, this poor e-classromm learning facilities factor may also influence any one country's distance learning students prefer . So, instead of whether the e-universities degrees courses contents are useful to let distance learning students to feel, whether the e-university's schoolf fees is cheap , whether the e-university's leacturers their past educational experiences, past educational personal quality and effort have more high level, whether the e-university had implemented this online degree course how long time, whether how may distance learning students had graduated for this online degree etc. factor. The e-university's internet technology facility may be one important technology resource factor to influence its anyone e-degree teaching course implement in success.

For this distance learning educational organization case, I assume that although the e-education organization has good educational experience teachers, one good courses design, but if it neglects how to provide excellent internet technology facility to let any one distance learning student to feel its any one e-classroom can provide easy person to person contact learning feeling, e.g. easy listen clealrly to any one e-teacher in any one e-classroom, easy enquires to any one e-teacher in any one e-classroom, easy to see any one teacher or student face in any one e-classroom, easy to communicate to any one e-student in any one e-classroom. Then, its any one different countries' distance learning students may feel its internet service facility can not provide excellent e-classroom leaning channel to let they feel. Then , they may choose another distance learning educational institute to replace very easily. Because any one distance learning student must need to install internet to link to the university's learning website to register to any one e-classroom, if the student's internet can not often link to the e-school's website easily, e.g. in this different learning situation, when one China e-learning student ofren feels that US e-university 's every e-classroom can link to his home's computer only half hour, then the US e-university e-classroom will sudden disappear to the China e-student home computer website easily. SO, the China e-student may feel difficult to learn from the US e-university every e-classroom because he must need to attempt to spend 10 to 20 minutes to click to the US e-university website to register to the e-classroom again. This e-univeristy's university internet sudden stopping linking feeling whcih may influence the China student to feel this US e-university neglects to consider its rapid and easy linking internet technology to let him to continue on learning every time e-course easily. Then, this e-university poor internet linking technology facility it will influence he chooses another US e-learning institure to replace this US e-learning institure. It does not considerate matter whether there are many different countries e-students , e.g. above 1000 number, they need to apply themselves homes internet to click to this US e-university's this e-classroom to cause internet internet traffic jam busy to influence any one e-student's home computer webwite can not keep long time internet links to this US e-university , e-classroom at the same time. Although, this US e-university's busy internet traffic jam issue may seem to be one small matter, to compare how to raise any one e-course content design, how to improve any one e-leacturer teaching skill or improve any one e-lecturer teaching skill or quality issues. However, if these different countries 1000 e-students, they have above 500 e-students number, they often feel busy internet traffic jam to influence they can keep long internet linking e-classroom time to this US e-educatoinal institute every day. If this e-course only began three months, they need to spend 20 minutes at least and they need to spend more than one time or more times at least to re link to this US e-university e-clasromm website again. Then, after three months, they can be influenced to choose another US e-education organization to replace this US e-education organization by this US e-school's busy internet traffic jam factor easily. Hence , any one distance learning educational institute must not neglect to consider how to avoid frequent internet traffic jam technology faciliity occurrence problem in order to let global any one e-student does not feel difficult to learn from their e-classrooms. Otherwise, they can choose another elearning institure, it can does not let them to ecounter any internet traffic jam challenge when they need to learn from its any one e-classroom any time.

On conclusion, e-learning internet facility service feeling to every e-student, it may be one kind of intangible technology resource to any one e-educational institute. Because " none any one busy internet traffic jam" e-classroom feeling , which may bring direct positive emotion impact to any one distance learning student to choose continue to learn from this e-education institure or choose another to replace it. So, efficient, rapid, none any busy internet traffic jam technological facility may be the most influential technological resource element to assist any one e-educational institure development in success.

FOURTEEN

ORGANIZATION TIME RESOURCE EFFICIENT SPENDING METHODS

● Is time limited resource to organizations?

Time is an often ignored but invaluable resource in any organizations. All activities be it procurement, production or product movement involve time within on its own is not measurable unless it is method against time. Time gives a time measure of how an organization performs efficiently and effectively. Is time an organizational resource?

Time is an infinite resource. If not properly managed in an organization, it can have a negative, impact on both employers' and employees' productivity. Organizations should ensure that workers are well equipped to manage time in their duties. So, time is one part to organizational resource , instead of organizational resources are all assets that production process. The four basic types of organizational resources are human , monetary, raw materials and capital. Organizational resources are combined , used and transferred into finished products during the production process. Hence, time is needed to spend time resources to cooperate other resources, e.g. human resources, financial resources, physical resources and information resources to do any activities, because any organizations activities must need to spend organizational time to carry on any organizational activities. Hence, if the organizations can use its daily time to arrange how different department employees how to work efficiently. Then, the organization can not waste its organizational any time resources within its organization because time is one kind of infinite and intangible organization asset. Any organizations ought not waste its any time resource.

In fact , in any organizations, organizational management views time is as a scarce resource that must be invested as effectively. An organizations time, in contrast, goes largely unmanaged. Although, phone calls, e-mails, instant messages etc. The ability to prioritise and schedule work is extremely desirable for any organization corporate . Indeed, organizations continually overcommit their employers resources. Limiting growth and innovation can be achieved easily, when the organization can manage its time how to use on the best condition, because progress and time tracking is available to support any organizational goal. In organizational studies, resource management is the efficient and the required data are the demands for various resources, forecast by time period into the future as far as is reasonable.

Is a business sense, the term " limited resources" can refer to a training organizations have had to evolve in a climate of how use evaluations to see what needs to change , if the organization feels time is not enough to use, so organizations need to ensure an members of team know their roles are the necessity of delivering on time and budget, seeing how great resource management to software and following resource management. Regardless of the approach and tools used, organizations must determine how to use role-based resources for long-term planning or when the specific resource is not enough to be used.

So, organizations need to learn how resource utilization with busy time/ available time. By establishing effective resource management or predict when inefficiently used resources within the organization and work. Organizational excellence framwwork (performance measurement) by learning and applying these concepts. Organizational any working time is money and it is best to plan for effective resource, but few organizations treata it thatway number of hours away from their families and friends.

So, any organizations need to calculate " utilization rate", the rate at which a resource is utilize, often used in regard to an employees' time , e.g. for project managers, time management is an essential skill at each of these specific components of time mangement.

Entertainment theme park resources supply and leisure player psychology relationship
● What are entertanment theme park intangible resource
● How intangible resource excites visitors entertainment need

Amusement , entertainment theme parks aim to provide good playing different kinds of lesiure facilities, and ocean fish performance shows to attract visitors to buy tickets to play lesiure activities when they are staying in the entertainment theme park. I assume that any entertainment theme park must need large lands resources to build the different kinds of entertainment machines facilities to let visitors to choose to play, as well as ocean parks can provide whales animals and human ocean peformance shows to let visitors to see their attraction whales animals performances.

So, enough land supply , it can let the theme park to build different kinds of entertainment machine facilities and ocen park to let many visitors have enough space to stay or walk in the entertainment theme park any time. Even, some theme park builds some hotels to let visitors to live several days, when they can not spend whole day to play all entertainment machine facilities. So, land resources must need , if the theme park needs to increase more different kinds of leisure mahcine facilities, it ought need to expand more leisure machine facilities and let visitors can increase number. So, they won't feel noise and crowd feeling. Because noise and crowd environment may influence some visitors feel discomfortable to enjoy to stay long time in the theme park. Then, it may bring negative lesiure emotion to these visitors.

So, any entertainment theme parks whether their land supply is enough to let it to build more different kinds of entertainment machine facilities and let many visitors can feel the entertainment theme park environment is quiest and not crowd environment factor may influence any visitors' staying time and enjoyment feeling to the theme park, instead of whether its leisure facility activities are attraction.

Entertainment theme park resources supply and leisure player psychology relationship

● What are entertanment theme park intangible resource

● How intangible resource excites visitors entertainment need

Amusement , entertainment theme parks aim to provide good playing different kinds of lesiure facilities, and ocean fish performance shows to attract visitors to buy tickets to play lesiure activities when they are staying in the entertainment theme park. I assume that any entertainment theme park must need large lands resources to build the different kinds of entertainment machines facilities to let visitors to choose to play, as well as ocean parks can provide whales animals and human ocean peformance shows to let visitors to see their attraction whales animals performances.

So, enough land supply , it can let the theme park to build different kinds of entertainment machine facilities and ocen park to let many visitors have enough space to stay or walk in the entertainment theme park any time. Even, some theme park builds some hotels to let visitors to live several days, when they can not spend whole day to play all entertainment machine facilities. So, land resources must need , if the theme park needs to increase more different kinds of leisure mahcine facilities, it ought need to expand more leisure machine facilities and let visitors can increase number. So, they won't feel noise and crowd feeling. Because noise and crowd environment may influence some visitors feel discomfortable to enjoy to stay long time in the theme park. Then, it may bring negative lesiure emotion to these visitors.

So, any entertainment theme parks whether their land supply is enough to let it to build more different kinds of entertainment machine facilities and let many visitors can feel the entertainment theme park environment is quiest and not crowd environment factor may influence any visitors' staying time and enjoyment feeling to the theme park, instead of whether its leisure facility activities are attraction. Hence, one attraction land supply to build different kinds of entertainment machine facilities and cean parks and hotels to let visitors can enjoy quiet and not crowd comfortable feeling when they are staying to play any these entertainment facilities inthe theme park.

Entertainment machine facilities will be theme park playing resources, they may include: flat rides, rotter coasters, railways, water rides, dark rides, ferries wheels, transport rides. All of these entertainment facilities their leisure attraction , they may influence lesiure consumer individual enjoyment feeling whether is more or less. So, a theme park is s place with attractions made up of rides, such is roller coasters and water rides. They ususally contain a selection of different types of rides, along with shops, restaurants, and other entertainment outlets.

Theme park cann be enjoyed by adules, teenagers and children. So, a successful theme park must can bring memorable attractions that people want to ride to see over and over again. Great attractions are inclusive and are not overly restrictive. They should have great stroy telling elements and put visitors into unique situations.

Future trends in the theme park industry, they ought concentrate all resources on these aspects: Changes in business models, e.g. it does not consider only entertainment facilities, it ought consider park comfortable environment feeling, e.g. more free, flower, animals, performance, natural environment, more dynamic pricing, changes in interactions between empllyees and guests.So, HRM front line service employee performance will influence whether visitors can feel friendly service feeling (home family feeling), more touchless technology and arificicial intelligence, robots technological resource will be one kind excited entertainment machine facilities to every visitor, they like to play robotic entertainment machines, fresh entertainment enjoyment feeling, more augumented and virtual reality in quest experience, changes in the food experience. So, restaurant food supply resource may bring good taste to excite visitors relas feeling when they feel hungry and they need to find restaurants to eat good taste food.

So, theme park entertainment family resource expenditure must be the highest, e.g. small waterparks can assist less than one million to build, but parks of this size are considered move as water playgrounds. Generally, waterparks , cost between $10 million and $40 million to build, indoor theme parks require on average $10 million to $30 million to build. So, the main resource element is the different kinds of entertainment facilities. Any kind of model of theme park needs to make decision whether which kind of enetertainment facility will be their theme park garden, e.g. water playground or indoor theme park, or natural environment forest enjoyment feeling, ocean park seeing whale performance show etc. theme park kinds. Because capital is limited. So, themem park designer needs to consider whether what kind of theme park feature is the most suitable to build in the land in order to avoid waste building land and not suitable entertainment facilities building material resources, when they can not attract many visitors to buy tickets to enter visit the theme park. For an amusement park example, it is a park that features various attractions, such as rides as well as other events for entertainmetn purposes. A theme park is a type of amusement park that bses its structures and attractions around a central theme, often featuring multiple areas with different themes. The others for amusement park may include: Theme park, carnival, funfair, pleasure ground, safari park, water park.

So, what kind features of theme park construction choice, it may influence future what lesiure needs for the visitors. Theme park investors need to gather fata to make market decision to choose to build what kinds of theme park in order to build what kinds of theme park in orde to attract the kind of leisure choice visitors.

for disney theme park exmample, it avoids birds play the sound in distress. It will there for keep birds away from visitors and allow for guests to eat in peace without being bothered by hungry birds. So, it increases resources for birds only. So, birds can have more gardens to let them to fly. They wont fly away the gardens in Desney. So, any gueses do not feel worry about the sound of birds in distress. Also, any theme parks need to invest resources on safety aspect when any one guest plays any kinds of entertainment facilities, e.g. the safest roller coaster is Blackpool, theme park. It can attract many guests to play its entertainment facilities. This theme park locates near to US one beach. Because , it did not cause any one guest dies before, when they go to US this beach, they will like to pay ticket to play rides entertainment facilities. Because it often spends expenditure on rides repairment aspect, so, it can bring the safest feeling to let any one beach guest feels leisure ride playing need when they visits to this US beach to feel swimming need. They also feel playing rides entertainment needs both. Hence, any kinds of theme park investors need to consider how to allocate limited resources to the different element aspect in order to safety, entertainment facilities attraction , reasonable price, enjoyment animals performance shows, restaurents good food taste providing hotel comfortable living feeling aims to all themem park guests.

Explaining the relationship between increasing proficient workers number and avoiding excess resource waste

● In organizational behavioral economic view, whether they have cause and effect relationship between employees how to use resources behaviors and organizational resource excess use within organizations ?

In organizational behavioral economic view, whether they have cause and effect relationship between employees how to use resources behaviors and organizational resource excess use within organizations. For example, if the organization has many employees number, whether the organization will use its any internal tangible and intangible resources easily per day.

For construction organization example, one construction organization must need to buy different kinds of construction materials to prepare to let workers to help it to manufacture different kinds of properties or houses (products) in order to sell to property buyers. In its every building construction site, it will need more or less workers, they are needed to use different kinds of construction materials to build housess in different construction sites. I assume that construction site (A), it has 100 construction workers number, every day, construction site (A) 100 workers need to use different kinds of construction materials to help them to build 3 building floors wall at least floor number in the construction site (A).

I assume that these 100 construction workers , they include proficient workers and not proficient workers. For proficient construction workers group, they have 50 number, and not proficient construction workers group, they also have 50 number . Hence, the proficient construction workers only need to spend 3 hours maximum and use less number of constructoin materials, then they can finish to build 3 building floors wall per day.

I also assume that all constructoin material supply number is limited. It means that due to this construction firm needs to pre-booking to purchase this kind of the best quality of constructoin material from overseas before three worths. So, it must not have enough time to pre-booking to purchase this kind of best quality of constructoin materials when they are used rapaidly within one month, due to this one month is the final finishing time to this construction firm within one month. Hence, limited construction material supply number and limited finishing time to build this new 40 floors house within this final one month .

So , not proficient construction workers number , limit number of construction material and per day 8 hours which is its limited resources in behavioral eocnomy view. Moreover, total 50 proficient and not proficient 50 construction workers (human resource employees number) will cause this constructoin firm , it will possible need to build this new 40 floors house are more than one month, if these 50 proficient construction workers , they have more than 30 at least number, they are absent to cause their overall construction workers' efficiency to be fallen down, due to the other 50 not proficient constuction numbers must need their teaching how to cooperate ad how use less materials to build this new 40 floor hourse rapidly in order to raise overall constructon team efficiency and avoid to delay more than one month time to build this 40 floors new house successfully within this final one month time.

Hence, it explains that when one organization has more employees, it does not represent that this organization must need to use more resource to achieve its any mission, such as this construction firm case, although it has 50 not proficient construction workers, they need to use more construction materials to build this new 40 floors house in this construction site (A). But, in fact, it has other 50 proficient construction workers, they know how to reduce construction materials to build every building floor wall for this new 40 floors building house. So, they can teach the not proficient building workers to know hoe to avoid to use extra excess constructon material to finish to construct every building fllor wall. SO, although, it has 50 not proficient construction workers number, but they can be taught to learn how to reduce to use these limited the best quality of construction materials to build this 40 floors new house. It implies that if the construction workers number can increase, e.g. increases more 50 not proficient construction workers, this the best quality of construction material resource number must not need to increase demand, because this construction site (A) has 50 proficient construction workers , they can teach these 50 not proficient construction workers how to avoid to use extra excess this kind of high quality construction material to build this new 40 floor house efficiently and effectively within this one month.

Hence, if this construction firm won't have more than 30 proficient workers number is absent in this final one month, it will have enough proficient construction workers to teach these 50 not proficient construction workers to know how to use this high quality of construction materials to build this 40 floors new house building in order to avoid waste or construction material need shortage challenge occurs in this final one month time.

Consequently , it ought finish to build this 40 floors new house building within this month. Hence, it explains why its this kind of high quality of construction material resource need must not increase, because if its all proficient construction workers is absent and their absent number is less than 30, then they have enough proficient construction workers number , they can teach this 50 not proficient construction workers how to avoid to use extra excess construction materials resource number in order to have enough construction material resource supply to satisfy this new 40 floors building house to finish construction within one month finishing date need.

On conclusion, in organizational behavioral economic view, it explains that resource use need must not be influenced to increase when the organization's employees number increase. It depends on whether the organization has how many talent and proficient workers number in order to assist them and teach the not proficient employees how to use resource to manufacture any kinds of products in order to avoid to spend extra excess of resource need. Hence, organizational behavioral economic view, it can explain that any organization's increase to employees number, it does not mean that its resource number is also needed to increase. Moreover, in organizational behavioral economic view, it also explains that if the organization can have many proficient workers to help it to do any complex tasks, they will help it to bring avoiding waste or excess extra resource to use advantage, because they ought know whether how they work, they can help the organization to improve performance or raise efficiency e.g. car manufacture, computer manufacture, television manufcture etc. home electronic products or car leisure products. Due to that manufacturre processes are complex, if the organization can have more proficient high skillful workers to help it to manufacture their products. They ought help it to use lesser manufacturing time and less manufacturing resource to finish any above these products to compare not proficient or low skillful manufacture workers. So, in long time, the organization must may earn economic low cost benefits from proficient worker individual high manufacturing skillful knowledge behavior or performance. So, organizational behavioral economic theory explains why even the organization plans to increase employees number, it's resources number won't be influenced to increase rapidly because when the organization's proficient high skillful workers number is more 2 times at least than not proficient low skillful workers number. They ought have enough effort to train and teach and cooperate with the not proficient low skillful manufacture workers to improve their manufacture skills in order to raise manufacturing efficiency and reduce extra excess resources waste and avoid to bring long term resource waste economic loss. So, any manufacturing organizations must need to increase proficient workers number to assist the not proficient low skillful workers to learn how to improve their skills and know how to reduce to use excess resources to keep to manufacture the highest number of products aim frequently. Consequently, the organization will bring long term low resource use manufacturing economic benefit.

How green building helps organizations to reduce resource waste

● green building avoids resource waste

The relationship between organization resource and earth resource in behavioral economic view, global organizations use any kinds of resource, such as office, warehouse facility building resource to build any new offices, warehouses, supermarkets, shopping centers, car parks, whether they can bring global building resources reducing number to satisfy human houses living needs, if one day building resources are facing any kinds building material is reducing number, but global applying steel, wood, brick etc. different kinds of building material number increases, when global population number is still increasingm any high houses' building materials need increase, even low wood houses' wood natural resource needs increase in order to let many people can live in the expensive wood houses. SO, it brings this question: Would wood, natural resource, steel, brick resource have shortage supply challenge, due to office, warehouse, shopping center,manufacturer, ther fixed assets number building need increases, but the same time, global houses need number also increases, when polulation increases? Can businessmen their fixed assets : offices , warehouse, shopping centers, factories, supermarkets, etc. building need bring negative impact to influence future human living house resource nu mber decreases?

I assume that global businessmen their offices, warehouses, shopping centers, hospitals, private school education organizations, supermarkets etc. business organizations their buildings number is sudden increasing high, due to many organizations can earn more profit to expand their businesses. So, they will need to spend much woods, steels, bricks etc. different kinds nature resources to build any high , height offices buildings in different countries. So, wood, steel brick etc. different kinds of offices building material need must also sudden be influenced to sudden increase by global business organizations increasing number. When global businesses organizations number increases, it will cause global high height offices number increases, because every business organizations must need to rent any building office to operate their businesses. If global has many new businesses are continue growing, they will influence offices building need in possibe, even for food business , e.g. supermarke, restaurant building material need will also increase, if the reestaurant can earn more profit, then it will need to expand itself restaurant vacancy floor to let many food customers do not need to spend long queue time to wait table in order to avoid to loss these food customers, even it will buy any shopping center location to build one or more than one restaurant to satisfy food customers need . So building material needs to the new restaurant design, it may decide to decorate all restaurant location, to feel food customers to feel more comfortable when they are sitting in its restaurant.SO, when the restaurant changes its inside design , it needs to find designers to buy any new building materials to design its restaurant to be new one in order to attract food customer choice.

I assume that global many old restaurants need to recorate their inside, or many global restaurants number increases, then any restaurants material natural resource need number may also be influenced to increase. Then, our earth building material resource for restaurants need will influence general office buildings material resource, shopping center building material resource decreases to supply. When, global many restaurants are needed to build, more building material resource is needed to be used build new restaurants or is needed to decorate to change old restaurants design . So, our earth will have much building material resources to be used to build new restaurants or they are be used to decorate the old restaurants design in order to change new restaurants design function. So, our earth building material natural resources for new or old restuarants , which must increase, when global has many restaurants need any kinds of building materials to be used to help them to build new or old restaurants. Then, they must influence natural resources of building material supply number to be reduced to satisfy any office building matierals user need, even any house building material user need, if global offices and houses number sudden increase. Consequently, due to global building material natural resource can not be produced rapidly in order to satisfy any office building, shopping center, house, supermarket etc. different kinds business organizations or private houses needs. Then, the natural resource of building resources shortage, it may influence any kinds of building material production price increases. It may influence global business organizations need to pay high price to rent office or build office, or build supermarket, or build shopping center, even any private houses prices increase, when global building material natural resource has no enough number to be supplied to satisfy builders' need in order to help any office, supermarket, shopping center, supermarket warehouse etc. business organization users to build their properties to operate their businesses. SO, these businessmen must need to spend much money for building expenditure, when they begin to do their businesses. Even, public or private house buyers also need to pay more expenditure to buy houses to live , when any kinds of building material price increases.

So, it explains why global business organizations number increases may influence global public or private houses prices increase, when our earth has no enough natural resource to be building matieral supplied to satisfy global construction properties development need. Finally, when global construction properties developers feel our earth building material natural resource encounters supply shortage challengem due to they need to pay higher price to buy any kinds of building material to help any business organizations to build their offices, restaurants, supermarkets, shopping centers, wareshouses etc. different fixed assets buildings or they need to ehlp any public or private houses buyers to build their houses. Consequently, any one businessmen or house livers must need to pay high price to buy any houses or offices , restaurants, hospitals etc. different buildings either to live or to use for business operations. Hence, it seems that they have chose resource supply surplus or shortage relationship between business organizations and private house buyers.

ON conclusion, I recommend that any business office buildings ought choose green buildings orrice, their advantages may include to avoid nature resource waste, improved indoor environment, quality of life , saving water, reduce , reuse, enhanced health, eco-friendly for life, reducing operational cost and maintenance , energy -efficient, non-renewable, vs renesable resource, keep it clean, protecting our ecosystem . Hence, green buildings can not only reduce or eliminate negative impacts on the environment, by using less water, energy, or natural resources.

Moreover, green buildings, or substainable design, is the practice of increasing the efficiency with wich buildings and their sites use energy , water and materials, and reducing impaction human health and the environments for lifecycle of a building. So, on environmental benefits of grren building aspect, it can enhance and protect bio-diversity and ecosystems , imprive air and water quality, reducing waste streams, conserve and restore natural resources, on economic benefits of green building aspect, it can reduce operating costs, improve occupant productiviity, enhance asset value and profits optimize life-cycle economic performance, on social bebefits of green building aspct, it can enhance occupant health and comfort, improve indoor air quality, minimize strain on local utility infrastracture, improve overall qualty of life.

Consequently, if any organizations can apply green building concept to design and build their offices, waterhouses, restaurants, shopping centers etc. different kinds of business green buildings, even ourselves houses design is chosen by green building concept. On behavioral economic view, green building concept is the best moethod to help us to reduce natural resource waste nowadays. Then, I beleive that our earth nature resources won't be easte easily.

- facility management helps organizations to avoid resource waste

Can facility management helps organizations to avoid resource waste? How waste management helps in productivity improvement? Waste management is more long term, which involves investment in new technology processes, product and training that can improve production efficiency and reduce waste in using least amount og materials to make and package the products can reduce the materials ,cost and waste.

Why the facility management of waste dosposal is important? When waste is disposed of or recycled in a safe, ethical and responsible manner, it helps reduce the negative impacts of the environment, ensuring that waste management procedures are carried our with regularly helps ensure the fewer waste materials go to the general waste system. som if any organizations can implement the most efficient facility management system, then it can help the organization's internal any building material to keep long ife time. When the organization can have the best building facility materials , it doed not need to spend much money to carry on repairment. Then, building resource cost must not often changed new, it's fised repairment or building material purchase expenditure must reduce as well as the organization's building materials do not waste easily.

Why does facility management help organization to reduce waste cost? This is because of a company can manage its waste properly, reduction in waste can help the company to reduce its cost. Waste minization is a set of processes and practices intended to help managers to see waste minimisation as a primary focus for most waste management strategies. It can reduce waste and usually much improves resources optimisation. Why is facility management software important for productivity? Can efficient facility management bring efficient resource management for organizations?

For organization, building efficiency is absolutely critical for reducing overhead and contributes directly to corporate green initiatives. Building efficiency also improves the operations of the business as whole, and it ensures that employees are able to work productivity in a comfortable environment. Beside having the potential to directly improve productivity, facility management can influence other of employees' lives that contribute to the overall output of an organization. FM can improve social interaction among colleges as well as enabling them to work in an effective, focuses and motivated manner. So, FM has close relationship to let organizations can use resources efficiently, even avoiding wastes resources ad reduces long term cost. Organizing maintanance, repairs and security of the building and premises. This protects employees and FM in organizations may include: claening offices, handware inspection and maintenance, environment health and safety, space management, efficient transportation space parking resource arrangement, operational efficient resources implemenation . So, facility management and efficient resource has relationship of a multiple disciplines to ensure functinality , comfort, safety and efficiency of the build environment by people, place, process and technology resource management.

Today, many organizaions recognize the importance of FM to efficiently manage its properties . Their data to increase productivity by FM, are heating and coolong tasks carried out efficiently? To meet organizations every day needs, some organizations require spaces , such as meeting rooms, or huddle spaces. Hence, facilities management and corporate real estate provisions are becoming increasing need, on efficient resource management business, goals in the most , effective, efficient are quitable way aspect, FM can optimize and implement solutions which fit the organization's trategic . FM aims to help offices, and building resources facilities empower orgsanizations to function at their most efficient and effective level to use their resources.

From manufacturing platns to healthcare facility boosting

efficiency is a goals logistics resource management is important to have proper organizatin policies in plan throughtout every facility. For example, high performance building, are characterized by their efficient use of resources and their ability to enhance the safety, health and productivity. So FM can help organizations to achieve to se resources in high performance effectiveness.

FM can also help organizations to save time. Any organizations must have offices to let employees can work together. If the organization lasks efficient and enough space to let many employees to feel comfortable to work together all working days. Their performance will be caused worse. So, efficient facility management to office rooms spaces, it can let employees to work in the most efficient manner.

Entertainment theme park resources supply and leisure player psychology relationship

● What are entertanment theme park intangible resource
● How intangible resource excites visitors entertainment need

Amusement , entertainment theme parks aim to provide good playing different kinds of lesiure facilities, and ocean fish performance shows to attract visitors to buy tickets to play lesiure activities when they are staying in the entertainment theme park. I assume that any entertainment theme park must need large lands resources to build the different kinds of entertainment machines facilities to let visitors to choose to play, as well as ocean parks can provide whales animals and human ocean peformance shows to let visitors to see their attraction whales animals performances.

So, enough land supply , it can let the theme park to build

different kinds of entertainment machine facilities and ocen park to let many visitors have enough space to stay or walk in the entertainment theme park any time. Even, some theme park builds some hotels to let visitors to live several days, when they can not spend whole day to play all entertainment machine facilities. So, land resources must need , if the theme park needs to increase more different kinds of leisure mahcine facilities, it ought need to expand more leisure machine facilities and let visitors can increase number. So, they won't feel noise and crowd feeling. Because noise and crowd environment may influence some visitors feel discomfortable to enjoy to stay long time in the theme park. Then, it may bring negative lesiure emotion to these visitors.

So, any entertainment theme parks whether their land supply is enough to let it to build more different kinds of entertainment machine facilities and let many visitors can feel the entertainment theme park environment is quiest and not crowd environment factor may influence any visitors' staying time and enjoyment feeling to the theme park, instead of whether its leisure facility activities are attraction. Hence, one attraction land supply to build different kinds of entertainment machine facilities and cean parks and hotels to let visitors can enjoy quiet and not crowd comfortable feeling when they are staying to play any these entertainment facilities inthe theme park.

Entertainment machine facilities will be theme park playing resources, they may include: flat rides, rotter coasters, railways, water rides, dark rides, ferries wheels, transport rides. All of these entertainment facilities their leisure attraction , they may influence lesiure consumer individual enjoyment feeling whether is more or less. So, a theme park is s place with attractions made up of rides, such is roller coasters and water rides. They ususally contain a selection of different types of rides, along with shops, restaurants, and other entertainment outlets.

Theme park cann be enjoyed by adules, teenagers and children. So, a successful theme park must can bring memorable attractions that people want to ride to see over and over again. Great attractions are inclusive and are not overly restrictive. They should have great stroy telling elements and put visitors into unique situations.

Future trends in the theme park industry, they ought concentrate all resources on these aspects: Changes in business models, e.g. it does not consider only entertainment facilities, it ought consider park comfortable environment feeling, e.g. more free, flower, animals, performance, natural environment, more dynamic pricing, changes in interactions between empllyees and guests.So, HRM front line service employee performance will influence whether visitors can feel friendly service feeling (home family feeling), more touchless technology and arificicial intelligence, robots technological resource will be one kind excited entertainment machine facilities to every visitor, they like to play robotic entertainment machines, fresh entertainment enjoyment feeling, more augumented and virtual reality in quest experience, changes in the food experience. So, restaurant food supply resource may bring good taste to excite visitors relas feeling when they feel hungry and they need to find restaurants to eat good taste food.

So, theme park entertainment family resource expenditure must be the highest, e.g. small waterparks can assist less than one million to build, but parks of this size are considered move as water playgrounds. Generally, waterparks , cost between $10 million and $40 million to build, indoor theme parks require on average $10 million to $30 million to build. So, the main resource element is the different kinds of entertainment facilities. Any kind of model of theme park needs to make decision whether which kind of enetertainment facility will be their theme park garden, e.g. water playground or indoor theme park, or natural environment forest enjoyment feeling, ocean park seeing whale performance show etc. theme park kinds. Because capital is limited. So, themem park designer needs to consider whether what kind of theme park feature is the most suitable to build in the land in order to avoid waste building land and not suitable entertainment facilities building material resources, when they can not attract many visitors to buy tickets to enter visit the theme park. For an amusement park example, it is a park that features various attractions, such as rides as well as other events for entertainmetn purposes. A theme park is a type of amusement park that bses its structures and attractions around a central theme, often featuring multiple areas with different themes. The others for amusement park may include: Theme park, carnival, funfair, pleasure ground, safari park, water park.

So, what kind features of theme park construction choice, it may influence future what lesiure needs for the visitors. Theme park investors need to gather fata to make market decision to choose to build what kinds of theme park in order to build what kinds of theme park in orde to attract the kind of leisure choice visitors.

for disney theme park exmample, it avoids birds play the sound in distress. It will there for keep birds away from visitors and allow for guests to eat in peace without being bothered by hungry birds. So, it increases resources for birds only. So, birds can have more gardens to let them to fly. They wont fly away the gardens in Desney. So, any gueses do not feel worry about the sound of birds in distress. Also, any theme parks need to invest resources on safety aspect when any one guest plays any kinds of entertainment facilities, e.g. the safest roller coaster is Blackpool, theme park. It can attract many guests to play its entertainment facilities. This theme park locates near to US one beach. Because , it did not cause any one guest dies before, when they go to US this beach, they will like to pay ticket to play rides entertainment facilities. Because it often spends expenditure on rides repairment aspect, so, it can bring the safest feeling to let any one beach guest feels leisure ride playing need when they visits to this US beach to feel swimming need. They also feel playing rides entertainment needs both. Hence, any kinds of theme park investors need to consider how to allocate limited resources to the different element aspect in order to safety, entertainment facilities attraction , reasonable price, enjoyment animals performance shows, restaurents good food taste providing hotel comfortable living feeling aims to all themem park guests.

Explaining the relationship between increasing proficient workers number and avoiding excess resource waste

● In organizational behavioral economic view, whether they have cause and effect relationship between employees how to use resources behaviors and organizational resource excess use within organizations ?

In organizational behavioral economic view, whether they have cause and effect relationship between employees how to use resources behaviors and organizational resource excess use within organizations. For example, if the organization has many employees number, whether the organization will use its any internal tangible and intangible resources easily per day.

For construction organization example, one construction organization must need to buy different kinds of construction materials to prepare to let workers to help it to manufacture different kinds of properties or houses (products) in order to sell to property buyers. In its every building construction site, it will need more or less workers, they are needed to use different kinds of construction materials to build housess in different construction sites. I assume that construction site (A), it has 100 construction workers number, every day, construction site (A) 100 workers need to use different kinds of construction materials to help them to build 3 building floors wall at least floor number in the construction site (A).

I assume that these 100 construction workers , they include proficient workers and not proficient workers. For proficient construction workers group, they have 50 number, and not proficient construction workers group, they also have 50 number . Hence, the proficient construction workers only need to spend 3 hours maximum and use less number of constructoin materials, then they can finish to build 3 building floors wall per day.

I also assume that all constructoin material supply number is limited. It means that due to this construction firm needs to pre-booking to purchase this kind of the best quality of constructoin material from overseas before three worths. So, it must not have enough time to pre-booking to purchase this kind of best quality of constructoin materials when they are used rapaidly within one month, due to this one month is the final finishing time to this construction firm within one month. Hence, limited construction material supply number and limited finishing time to build this new 40 floors house within this final one month .

So , not proficient construction workers number , limit number of construction material and per day 8 hours which is its limited resources in behavioral eocnomy view. Moreover, total 50 proficient and not proficient 50 construction workers (human resource employees number) will cause this constructoin firm , it will possible need to build this new 40 floors house are more than one month, if these 50 proficient construction workers , they have more than 30 at least number, they are absent to cause their overall construction workers' efficiency to be fallen down, due to the other 50 not proficient constuction numbers must need their teaching how to cooperate ad how use less materials to build this new 40 floor hourse rapidly in order to raise overall constructon team efficiency and avoid to delay more than one month time to build this 40 floors new house successfully within this final one month time.

Hence, it explains that when one organization has more employees, it does not represent that this organization must need to use more resource to achieve its any mission, such as this construction firm case, although it has 50 not proficient construction workers, they need to use more construction materials to build this new 40 floors house in this construction site (A). But, in fact, it has other 50 proficient construction workers, they know how to reduce construction materials to build every building floor wall for this new 40 floors building house. So, they can teach the not proficient building workers to know hoe to avoid to use extra excess constructon material to finish to construct every building fllor wall. SO, although, it has 50 not proficient construction workers number, but they can be taught to learn how to reduce to use these limited the best quality of construction materials to build this 40 floors new house. It implies that if the construction workers number can increase, e.g. increases more 50 not proficient construction workers, this the best quality of construction material resource number must not need to increase demand, because this construction site (A) has 50 proficient construction workers , they can teach these 50 not proficient construction workers how to avoid to use extra excess this kind of high quality construction material to build this new 40 floor house efficiently and effectively within this one month.

Hence, if this construction firm won't have more than 30 proficient workers number is absent in this final one month, it will have enough proficient construction workers to teach these 50 not proficient construction workers to know how to use this high quality of construction materials to build this 40 floors new house building in order to avoid waste or construction material need shortage challenge occurs in this final one month time.

Consequently , it ought finish to build this 40 floors new house building within this month. Hence, it explains why its this kind of high quality of construction material resource need must not increase, because if its all proficient construction workers is absent and their absent number is less than 30, then they have enough proficient construction workers number , they can teach this 50 not proficient construction workers how to avoid to use extra excess construction materials resource number in order to have enough construction material resource supply to satisfy this new 40 floors building house to finish construction within one month finishing date need.

On conclusion, in organizational behavioral economic view, it explains that resource use need must not be influenced to increase when the organization's employees number increase. It depends on whether the organization has how many talent and proficient workers number in order to assist them and teach the not proficient employees how to use resource to manufacture any kinds of products in order to avoid to spend extra excess of resource need. Hence, organizational behavioral economic view, it can explain that any organization's increase to employees number, it does not mean that its resource number is also needed to increase. Moreover, in organizational behavioral economic view, it also explains that if the organization can have many proficient workers to help it to do any complex tasks, they will help it to bring avoiding waste or excess extra resource to use advantage, because they ought know whether how they work, they can help the organization to improve performance or raise efficiency e.g. car manufacture, computer manufacture, television manufcture etc. home electronic products or car leisure products. Due to that manufacturre processes are complex, if the organization can have more proficient high skillful workers to help it to manufacture their products. They ought help it to use lesser manufacturing time and less manufacturing resource to finish any above these products to compare not proficient or low skillful manufacture workers. So, in long time, the organization must may earn economic low cost benefits from proficient worker individual high manufacturing skillful knowledge behavior or performance. So, organizational behavioral economic theory explains why even the organization plans to increase employees number, it's resources number won't be influenced to increase rapidly because when the organization's proficient high skillful workers number is more 2 times at least than not proficient low skillful workers number. They ought have enough effort to train and teach and cooperate with the not proficient low skillful manufacture workers to improve their manufacture skills in order to raise manufacturing efficiency and reduce extra excess resources waste and avoid to bring long term resource waste economic loss. So, any manufacturing organizations must need to increase proficient workers number to assist the not proficient low skillful workers to learn how to improve their skills and know how to reduce to use excess resources to keep to manufacture the highest number of products aim frequently. Consequently, the organization will bring long term low resource use manufacturing economic benefit. How organization resource influences

earth resource shortage

How green building helps organizations to reduce resource waste

● green building avoids resource waste

The relationship between organization resource and earth resource in behavioral economic view, global organizations use any kinds of resource, such as office, warehouse facility building resource to build any new offices, warehouses, supermarkets, shopping centers, car parks, whether they can bring global building resources reducing number to satisfy human houses living needs, if one day building resources are facing any kinds building material is reducing number, but global applying steel, wood, brick etc. different kinds of building material number increases, when global population number is still increasingm any high houses' building materials need increase, even low wood houses' wood natural resource needs increase in order to let many people can live in the expensive wood houses. SO, it brings this question: Would wood, natural resource, steel, brick resource have shortage supply challenge, due to office, warehouse, shopping center,manufacturer, ther fixed assets number building need increases, but the same time, global houses need number also increases, when polulation increases? Can businessmen their fixed assets : offices , warehouse, shopping centers, factories, supermarkets, etc. building need bring negative impact to influence future human living house resource nu mber decreases?

I assume that global businessmen their offices, warehouses, shopping centers, hospitals, private school education organizations, supermarkets etc. business organizations their buildings number is sudden increasing high, due to many organizations can earn more profit to expand their businesses. So, they will need to spend much woods, steels, bricks etc. different kinds nature resources to build any high , height offices buildings in different countries. So, wood, steel brick etc. different kinds of offices building material need must also sudden be influenced to sudden increase by global business organizations increasing number. When global businesses organizations number increases, it will cause global high height offices number increases, because every business organizations must need to rent any building office to operate their businesses. If global has many new businesses are continue growing, they will influence offices building need in possibe, even for food business , e.g. supermarke, restaurant building material need will also increase, if the reestaurant can earn more profit, then it will need to expand itself restaurant vacancy floor to let many food customers do not need to spend long queue time to wait table in order to avoid to loss these food customers, even it will buy any shopping center location to build one or more than one restaurant to satisfy food customers need . So building material needs to the new restaurant design, it may decide to decorate all restaurant location, to feel food customers to feel more comfortable when they are sitting in its restaurant.SO, when the restaurant changes its inside design , it needs to find designers to buy any new building materials to design its restaurant to be new one in order to attract food customer choice.

I assume that global many old restaurants need to recorate their inside, or many global restaurants number increases, then any restaurants material natural resource need number may also be influenced to increase. Then, our earth building material resource for restaurants need will influence general office buildings material resource, shopping center building material resource decreases to supply. When, global many restaurants are needed to build, more building material resource is needed to be used build new restaurants or is needed to decorate to change old restaurants design . So, our earth will have much building material resources to be used to build new restaurants or they are be used to decorate the old restaurants design in order to change new restaurants design function. So, our earth building material natural resources for new or old restuarants , which must increase, when global has many restaurants need any kinds of building materials to be used to help them to build new or old restaurants. Then, they must influence natural resources of building material supply number to be reduced to satisfy any office building matierals user need, even any house building material user need, if global offices and houses number sudden increase. Consequently, due to global building material natural resource can not be produced rapidly in order to satisfy any office building, shopping center, house, supermarket etc.

different kinds business organizations or private houses needs. Then, the natural resource of building resources shortage, it may influence any kinds of building material production price increases. It may influence global business organizations need to pay high price to rent office or build office, or build supermarket, or build shopping center, even any private houses prices increase, when global building material natural resource has no enough number to be supplied to satisfy builders' need in order to help any office, supermarket, shopping center, supermarket warehouse etc. business organization users to build their properties to operate their businesses. SO, these businessmen must need to spend much money for building expenditure, when they begin to do their businesses. Even, public or private house buyers also need to pay more expenditure to buy houses to live , when any kinds of building material price increases.

So, it explains why global business organizations number increases may influence global public or private houses prices increase, when our earth has no enough natural resource to be building matieral supplied to satisfy global construction properties development need. Finally, when global construction properties developers feel our earth building material natural resource encounters supply shortage challengem due to they need to pay higher price to buy any kinds of building material to help any business organizations to build their offices, restaurants, supermarkets, shopping centers, wareshouses etc. different fixed assets buildings or they need to ehlp any public or private houses buyers to build their houses. Consequently, any one businessmen or house livers must need to pay high price to buy any houses or offices , restaurants, hospitals etc. different buildings either to live or to use for business operations. Hence, it seems that they have chose resource supply surplus or shortage relationship between business organizations and private house buyers.

ON conclusion, I recommend that any business office buildings ought choose green buildings orrice, their advantages may include to avoid nature resource waste, improved indoor environment, quality of life , saving water, reduce , reuse, enhanced health, eco-friendly for life, reducing operational cost and maintenance , energy -efficient, non-renewable, vs renesable resource, keep it clean, protecting our ecosystem . Hence, green buildings can not only reduce or eliminate negative impacts on the environment, by using less water, energy, or natural resources.

Moreover, green buildings, or substainable design, is the practice of increasing the efficiency with wich buildings and their sites use energy , water and materials, and reducing impaction human health and the environments for lifecycle of a building. So, on environmental benefits of grren building aspect, it can enhance and protect bio-diversity and ecosystems , imprive air and water quality, reducing waste streams, conserve and restore natural resources, on economic benefits of green building aspect, it can reduce operating costs, improve occupant productiviity, enhance asset value and profits optimize life-cycle economic performance, on social bebefits of green building aspct, it can enhance occupant health and comfort, improve indoor air quality, minimize strain on local utility infrastracture, improve overall qualty of life.

Consequently, if any organizations can apply green building concept to design and build their offices, waterhouses, restaurants, shopping centers etc. different kinds of business green buildings, even ourselves houses design is chosen by green building concept. On behavioral economic view, green building concept is the best moethod to help us to reduce natural resource waste nowadays. Then, I beleive that our earth nature resources won't be easte easily.

● facility management helps organizations to avoid resource waste

Can facility management helps organizations to avoid resource waste? How waste management helps in productivity improvement? Waste management is more long term, which involves investment in new technology processes, product and training that can improve production efficiency and reduce waste in using least amount og materials to make and package the products can reduce the materials ,cost and waste.

Why the facility management of waste dosposal is important? When waste is disposed of or recycled in a safe, ethical and responsible manner, it helps reduce the negative impacts of the environment, ensuring that waste management procedures are carried our with regularly helps ensure the fewer waste materials go to the general waste system. som if any organizations can implement the most efficient facility management system, then it can help the organization's internal any building material to keep long ife time. When the organization can have the best building facility materials , it doed not need to spend much money to carry on repairment. Then, building resource cost must not often changed new, it's fised repairment or building material purchase expenditure must reduce as well as the organization's building materials do not waste easily.

Why does facility management help organization to reduce waste cost? This is because of a company can manage its waste properly, reduction in waste can help the company to reduce its cost. Waste minization is a set of processes and practices intended to help managers to see waste minimisation as a primary focus for most waste management strategies. It can reduce waste and usually much improves resources optimisation. Why is facility management software important for productivity? Can efficient facility management bring efficient resource management for organizations?

For organization, building efficiency is absolutely critical for reducing overhead and contributes directly to corporate green initiatives. Building efficiency also improves the operations of the business as whole, and it ensures that employees are able to work productivity in a comfortable environment. Beside having the potential to directly improve productivity, facility management can influence other of employees' lives that contribute to the overall output of an organization. FM can improve social interaction among colleges as well as enabling them to work in an effective, focuses and motivated manner. So, FM has close relationship to let organizations can use resources efficiently, even avoiding wastes resources ad reduces long term cost. Organizing maintanance, repairs and security of the building and premises. This protects employees and FM in organizations may include: claening offices, handware inspection and maintenance, environment health and safety, space management, efficient transportation space parking resource arrangement, operational efficient resources implemenation . So, facility management and efficient resource has relationship of a multiple disciplines to ensure functinality , comfort, safety and efficiency of the build environment by people, place, process and technology resource management.

Today, many organizaions recognize the importance of FM to efficiently manage its properties . Their data to increase productivity by FM, are heating and coolong tasks carried out efficiently? To meet organizations every day needs, some organizations require spaces , such as meeting rooms, or huddle spaces. Hence, facilities management and corporate real estate provisions are becoming increasing need, on efficient resource management business, goals in the most , effective, efficient are quitable way aspect, FM can optimize and implement solutions which fit the organization's trategic . FM aims to help offices, and building resources facilities empower orgsanizations to function at their most efficient and effective level to use their resources.

From manufacturing platns to healthcare facility boosting efficiency is a goals logistics resource management is important to have proper organizatin policies in plan throughtout every facility. For example, high performance building, are characterized by their efficient use of resources and their ability to enhance the safety, health and productivity. So FM can help organizations to achieve to se resources in high performance effectiveness.

FM can also help organizations to save time. Any organizations must have offices to let employees can work together. If the organization lasks efficient and enough space to let many employees to feel comfortable to work together all working days. Their performance will be caused worse. So, efficient facility management to office rooms spaces, it can let employees to work in the most efficient manner.